SIGNS

Sacred Encounters with Pathways,
Turning Points, and Divine Guideposts

Enjoy these other books in the Common Sentience series:

ANCESTORS: *Divine Remembrances of Lineage, Relations and Sacred Sites*

ANGELS: *Personal Encounters with Divine Beings of Light*

ANIMALS: *Personal Tales of Encounters with Spirit Animals*

ASCENSION: *Divine Stories of Awakening the Whole and Holy Being Within*

GUIDES: *Mystical Connections to Soul Guides and Divine Teachers*

MEDITATION: *Intimate Experiences with the Divine through Contemplative Practices*

NATURE: *Divine Experiences with Trees, Plants, Stones and Landscapes*

SHAMANISM: *Personal Quests of Communion with Nature and Creation*

SOUND: *Profound Experiences with Chanting, Toning, Music and Healing Frequencies*

Learn more at sacredstories.com.

SIGNS

*Sacred Encounters with Pathways,
Turning Points, and Divine Guideposts*

SIMRAN

SACRED STORIES
PUBLISHING

Books may be purchased through booksellers or by contacting Sacred Stories Publishing.

Signs: Sacred Encounters with Pathways, Turning Points, and Divine Guideposts

SIMRAN

Print ISBN: 978-1-958921-19-7
EBook ISBN: 978-1-958921-20-3

Library of Congress Control Number: 2023931322

Published by Sacred Stories Publishing, Fort Lauderdale, FL USA

CONTENTS

PART THREE: DEEPENING YOUR CONNECTION WITH THE COSMOS

MEET OUR SACRED STORYTELLERS
MEET OUR FEATURED AUTHOR

PART ONE

Understanding Signs

You are the world and the world is you.

— KRISHNAMURTI

JOURNEY OF THE SOUL

a unique and beautiful story is unfolding all around you—and you might not know it.

You happened upon *Signs* because this book called to you. This was a "sign." You might have also been encountering other moments that seem implausible.

Signs that appear to you might be puzzling if they seem linked to things you have pondered, dreamed, or wished for. They could be related to challenges you are facing, and praying about. It is possible that you are questioning reality, or even your sanity. You may ask if others experience similar things—or you might stay quiet, feeling timid about what is happening in your world.

Within these pages is an opportunity to discover the guidance provided by signs. This book not only introduces you to various expressions of these sacred encounters, but also offers profound individual experiences that can expand your awareness, connection, and understanding of a world within your world.

Signs provides information, training, and confirmation for engaging a deeper experience with the situations you are encountering. You will learn that signs are not only present, but an ongoing and available resource for anyone who is ready to converse with the universe. Let these pages become a source of comfort, insight, and inspiration for embracing life in a more intimate and adventurous manner.

To recognize that signs are appearing for you, it is important to know why they exist, where they began, their purpose, and how they appear. It is also necessary to strengthen your ability to receive and discern what your signs are saying to you.

In this book, you'll find stories from others who have encountered their own signs. Their vignettes of experience illustrate sacred encounters that brought forth turning points which led them down their unique paths. Signs are Divine guideposts that lead to soul expansion and personal dharma.

Your signs do the same, if you are willing to see beyond the surface of life and your mind's skepticism. Your ever-deepening inquiry of signs will enfold you in delight, innocence, and a cascade of remembering. These are experienced when you see individual signs, and later as you connect the dots that weave across spans of time.

Finally, as you make your way through this text, I will provide my own string of experiences as an example of how signs connect to create an ongoing dialogue. This will help you understand how to better intuit signs, their broader meanings, and the integration process that I use. My method has opened me to the experience of signs showering upon my life.

Throughout the text, you might notice certain things are repeated. The purpose of this is two-fold. First, it serves as an illustration for how signs continually tap you on the shoulder. Repetition is a key characteristic of signs. Signs repeat to re-"mind" you, so that your perception and perspectives expand. Second, you have been conditioned to perceive the world in a logical and practical way. Signs are, by nature, neither logical nor practical. They are mystical, magical, and playful.

You are embarking on an intimate spiritual journey. After reading this book, you will never look at life in the same way. Trust your intuition as you follow in the direction life has pointed. When you hear the universe speak to you, your inner and outer dialogue reflects the new texture of experience. In time, signs will feel like words. Linking these words will create full sentences. With time and experience, the sentences become full paragraphs. They become conversations with the universe.

Life is not only connected, but also interconnected and reflective. It is a web that mirrors you. Life guides you. It speaks to you, about you. Pause for a moment and reflect upon how a flower, insect, animal, or person might have appeared to you as a sign. You are every part of the world, and it is speaking back to you about you. You are the universe, and the universe is you.

Create an intimate relationship with every sacred encounter, and let that intimacy expand your experience. Receiving signs can increase your awareness and expression of authenticity, personal power, and purpose. These messages, intended just for you, might reveal major life pivots, new roads, and empowering choices. Let your signs become pointers, your pointers become insight, your insight become integration, and let that integration move you toward inspired action.

Have a sacred encounter. Experience a turning point. Embark upon a purposeful pathway. Embrace your unique messages as Divine guideposts. In doing so, you will be led through the most marvelous and mystical experiences of your soul. This is the perfect moment to become present to your sacred encounters and open to your unique conversation with the universe. A beautiful human saga, filled with signs, is available for you. It encapsulates the journey of the soul in a most beautiful way.

But first, you may wonder why signs exist, and what happened that brought them forward. Let's begin...

CHILD'S PLAY

We are born of the cosmos. Every human being arrives wide-eyed with wonder, draped in innocence yet rich with other-worldly wisdom. We can observe this within an infant's eyes. The magnificence of God is palpable in a newborn baby.

Infants are sponges, taking in the world at warp speed. They grow and change with every sight, smell, sound, taste, and touch. Not realizing that the child came to remind them of the truth they have forgotten, caregivers teach and model behavior based upon their own beliefs and fears about life. Unaware that the child came as a sign for the parent, the child is unknowingly exposed to beliefs and polarities held by them. This will undoubtedly create wounding in the child that echoes that of the parent.

An echo is a rhythmic ping that repeats until awareness returns for awakening. The echo is the rippling of a sign. This is how contrast, distortion, duality, and dissonance become infused into each of our lives. Children absorb information on many levels—cognitively, energetically, emotionally, physically, and intuitively—and then begin creating experiences that replicate what was modeled, repressed, and carried.

In time, the child's imagination and playfulness—as well as their dreams—conform to their environment and to the size and shape of the caregiver's perceptions as they establish their own identity. In adolescence and early adulthood, the child's identity also begins to reflect all the ancestry that came before.

Children quickly learn the importance of playing by others' spoken and unspoken rules. They begin to absorb the constructs of education, religion, and media. This ongoing conditioning solidifies their beliefs including their thoughts around success and destiny. Eventually, the original innocence is forgotten.

Early childhood predispositions bring about a living framework that shapes, limits, confines, and constricts what was once limitless, boundless, and free. This draws us farther out into the external. Yet it is also what sets in motion the string of signs that begin appearing when ready to receive them. Through the outer world, we begin finding our way back from forgetting.

Forgetting is unavoidable, since conditioning begins in infancy. The once-wide-open heart is now guarded. A deep connection to sacred gives way to a multiplicity of masks, patterns, and behaviors.

Where there was once oneness of mind, heart, and spirit, now a feeling of separation develops and the being experiences duality and discord.

Awareness of essence moves into sublayers of the body, mind, and heart. Source is projected out into the universe. The natural creative capacity is perceived as distant and inaccessible.

Survival becomes the priority. The shadow self forms. It is the hidden twin of the 'child self'. This is the part of you that eventually creates the obstacles and challenges, urging you to remember and reclaim your essence. The shadow creates moments of discord for your greater good, although it may not feel that way. These moments of contrast can be viewed as unorthodox signs. They bubble up so that you begin asking questions and seeking answers.

Your early life determines which of the six core human wounds develop: repression, denial, shame, rejection, guilt, and separation. In a roundabout way, your core wounds will eventually return you to mysticism, magic, and miracles. Signs begin appearing as a means of pointing toward what you are destined to remember, if you are open, available, and receptive.

This storyline is the same for each of us. No matter what your family of origin was, a version of this process occurred. Even if you are awake and aware, you are passing belief systems and ways of seeing the world onto those in your care. Every human being is part of the human condition; each one must take the journey of the soul.

THE YELLOW BRICK ROAD

Life is temporal and mire-filled but also magical. Within the constructs built from childhood, the golden thread of essence weaves its way upward, entwining your daily experiences with life's sacred mystery.

What occurred throughout your younger years flips to a new mission: awakening. The inner child and your essence, in partnership, construct a way back to your true self. Just as Dorothy did in the *Wizard of Oz*, you will encounter people, places and things that will uproot your fears, create turnarounds, and deepen your faith as you travel this yellow brick road. Your return home becomes an adventure involving your own, intimate relationships with courage, mind mastery, and opening your heart.

Even the mundane will hold hidden treasures and special keys to awareness, transformation, and alchemy. The hero's journey that then unfolds is an exciting opportunity for discovery and recovery.

Your greatest challenge will be your "self," encumbered by identity, wounding, and doubt. You will search for the ability to reconnect human experience to mystical nature. However, during this time, you are likely to perceive more questions than answers. You won't yet realize that the answers *are* the questions. Your search will not only lead you forward, but also allow you to access the signs that have long surrounded you.

The journey of a lifetime begins within a darkened tunnel of age-old questions. "Why am I here? Is this all there is? What is my purpose?" When you venture into this tunnel, your vision expands so that you notice signs, symbols, and synchronicities. At the same time, you will recognize the smallness of the self and will begin the process of releasing everything you've taken on through conditioning.

"It is always darkest before dawn." This is true for the journey as a human. Within the darkness of confusion, psychosis, and "dark nights of the soul," your shadows rear up. These squatters have been waiting for the right time to plant their discordant experiences. Their mission is to uproot everything false about your life. Your world going topsy-turvy may not feel good, but it does open you to a new world.

Letting go of what you have become requires releasing what you know. Most of us don't do this willingly. For that reason, the universe conspires to bring forth a multitude of signs that reveal internal and external direction, areas calling for change, and sparks of Divine presence. Unfolding events may seem climactic, and at times chaotic, but they are also cosmic. Your life will orchestrate a series of events, meetings, and signs that support you in letting go so you can experience something greater. Life helps you embark upon a walk of infinite mastery. You need only follow the signs. They are your "Yellow Brick Road" home.

THE JOURNEY AS YOU

We experience the world in a multitude of ways. Our senses help us translate theoretical learning into integrated awareness. Human beings also have shape-shifting qualities. The journey you take *as you* is a sensory and extra-sensory experience. Your YES becomes vitally important for experiencing the mystical.

Your body is the bridge between where you are and where your soul intends for you to go. The senses connect to and receive mystical experience in ways that the conscious mind cannot, through intuitive knowing.

Although the five senses play a significant role in perception, the "journey as you" expands beyond your body. As you begin the return home to your true self, you will uncover the subtler realms of your senses once again, and signs will use the senses to get your attention.

You also possess extra-sensory perception, known as the sixth sense, which allows you to see and know things beyond intellectual understanding.

This Divine intelligence helps you interpret the world in a metaphysical manner. In strengthening your sixth sense, you open to the field of knowing. This sense accesses the mystical aspects of life that sit within the ordinary and humdrum. You are then able to see the inner workings of the world, and understand life in a brand new way. This innate, intuitive quality will allow you to recognize more signs.

SACRED ENCOUNTERS

Life is filled with the mystical… the magical… and the magnificent. Trust your eyes, your ears, and your sensations. The universe is talking to you. Signs are sacred encounters. They are pings. They exist as in-the-moment miracles. Signs are available to everyone, and each type guides us in a specific way. Pathways open when required. Turning points are necessary. Signs are everywhere.

DIVINE GUIDEPOSTS

The signs sprinkled along your path might be Divine guideposts. They are synchronistic moments where something of meaning appears to guide you. These glimpses open the eyes and ears to the Divine in life. Divine guideposts are flashes that come to produce insight, confirmation, and connection. They appear when needed and can occur randomly, daily, and throughout the day.

Divine guideposts comfort the heart, ease the mind, and can settle a restless spirit, relieving your anxiety. These signs will leave you speechless and filled with gratitude. Divine guideposts also show up to remind us of things that we have forgotten. They bring about "Aha!" moments to promote healing and closure.

A grieving woman drives to her deceased husband's favorite place. She sits on the bench where he used to sit and mourns him. Suddenly, a bright red cardinal perches nearby. This provides comfort. Before transitioning, her husband had shared that she should watch for cardinals.

An elderly man must pick up medicine from a busy pharmacy. He has difficulty walking, especially longer distances. The pharmacy is in a shopping center with a huge and typically full parking lot. He is aware that he may have to walk a great distance. On the drive there, he imagines easily slipping into a parking space close to the front. He holds the image in his mind and feels the satisfaction of it. As he pulls into the shopping center, a woman exiting the pharmacy catches his eye and points to her car, which is parked in the first space beyond handicap parking. She pulls out of the space and motions for him to park in the spot. He feels grateful to be so close to the pharmacy entrance.

Stacy moved back to her parents' farm after decades away. It had been willed to her upon her father's passing. Her mother had died when she was five years old. Feeling the loss of both parents deeply, she felt very alone in the home on her first night back. In her father's bedroom was a photograph of her parents together. She spoke to them through her tears. "Why did you have to leave?"

As she wiped her eyes, she noticed her mother was wearing a distinctive ring, a gift from her husband that she had subsequently lost years ago. Stacy found herself wishing she had the ring. As she placed the photograph back on her father's nightstand, that evening's full moon broke through the clouds, lighting the back yard in a peculiar way. A moonbeam illuminated the corner that had held her childhood sandbox.

Stacy followed the beam and knelt on the ground, where she spotted something shiny in the dirt: her mother's lost diamond ring. Stacy had played here countless times throughout her childhood. Why had the ring now appeared? Finding the ring helped Stacey realized that her mother and father were still with her, always nearby. She slid the ring on her finger, knowing she would never be alone.

PATHWAYS

Certain life questions are common. These typically have to do with direction, destiny, and purpose. "What is my life purpose? What should I do with my life? Where do I need to live? How did I get here? Where do I go from here?"

These questions serve as invitations for pathways to begin appearing in your life. The curious mind opens doorways of communication with the cosmos. There is power in the word. Sometimes, your mind or ego will choose a path, when your heart and soul desire something different. In this case, the path chosen by ego will ultimately redirect to paths that your heart and soul desire. Nothing is ever lost in translation. There are many ways to end up on your correct, Divinely ordained path.

Some of us have ambitions to become famous, wealthy, loved, skilled, holy, or wise. Others have specific and detailed aims, such as a certain career, lifestyle, or experience. Most people also live with the desire for purpose, even if the purpose is enjoyment and entertainment. In other cases, purpose relates to significance and self-value. Regardless of your purpose, signs will help you clarify and fine-tune this so that experience and expression lead you to the fullness of life.

Pathways enable us to ascend. Daily choices lead down roads of experience that shape and hone you. It is by your own invitation that the way is made. Then, via life's hand, new pathways will appear that continually realign your steps toward the soul's directive. In walking the pathways that appear, you develop trust, strength, and the possibility of transcending who you were before. Pathways lead to growth and mastery.

Jenna had no idea where to move after quitting her job. She wanted to create a balanced lifestyle after working in the corporate world for so many years. Life in big business had left little time for love, children or having fun. At the age of forty-eight, she believed it was too late for her to have children. Her body was exhausted and the cross-country trip she had embarked upon was feeding her soul.

While driving, she began daydreaming about a man riding in on a white horse, picking her up, and taking her to the most beautiful home. This dream was easy to sink into and she used it often, each time feeling the beauty of it more intensely.

A few hours later, her car signaled that the left tire was losing air. She prayed she would make it to the next exit, which was about thirty miles ahead. Twenty miles later, she found herself stranded on the side of the highway, five miles short of the exit.

A white convertible pulled up behind her. The friendly driver helped her contact a local towing service. She learned she would have to remain in the small town for a week until her car could be fixed. Dan, the driver of the white convertible, waited with her until the tow-truck arrived, and they had a wonderful conversation.

Dan offered to drive her to a local bed and breakfast where she could wait while her car was being fixed. She agreed. As they approached the exit, Jenna saw a sign that said, "Welcome to Hometown." She felt a flutter within her heart.

She soon discovered she and Dan had a lot in common. He had also left corporate America earlier in the year and, while on a road trip, had landed in Hometown, Pennsylvania. Ironically, he'd also had a flat tire near the exit. That was what made him stop for her. Seeing her in that situation made him feel grateful for where he now lived.

Before dropping her off, Dan invited Jenna out to dinner. One year later, she and Dan were married. He was a widower raising two young daughters. Today, ten years later, they enjoy their home, which is nestled amidst rolling hills and green pastures. Jenna has horses and loves to sit by her pond. Jenna's daydream had come true. The flat tire and her willingness to remain open to possibility created the pathway that led to her desired destiny.

TURNING POINTS

Turning points happen when you need, or are looking for, a new direction. They also occur when the universe is leveling-up your clarity, focus and vibration. A turning point is often a time of profound change. These moments end beneficially, but they can be filled with bumps along the way. This turbulence helps in clearing inner and outer obstacles. Some turning points are clear, and changes are made with conscious awareness and ease. Other times, turning points are monumental moments, turning your world upside down. Although these can create stress, temporary hardship, and panic, they also bring the opportunity for greater self-mastery.

A turning point might also arise as an epiphany, a vision, or a gentle nudge. The universe can shake up your life, unmistakably shove you forward, or use a "spiritual two-by-four" to wake you up. Regardless of which version you experience, turning points are transformative. In most cases, you will find yourself at a crossroads. You will undergo a change in direction and see new choices offered. Turning points catalyze decisions, supporting you in shifting and responding in ways that are more aligned. In many cases, a turning point is the beginning of your life completely changing. Although these experiences might feel like a complete mess, in time, you will realize that miracles unfolded.

June sat in the living room amidst boxes. The home she treasured was now a place of pain. Her husband had left her for another woman. With the process of divorce and a loss of identity, June realized she had been living her life for him. She had given up her dreams for her husband's career. She let go of her desires to fulfill his needs. June had given up her outgoing personality and freedom for his schedule and ambitions.

Looking around the room, June realized that the beautiful home had been a gilded cage that had kept her wound and bound. She lived a lush lifestyle, but none of it held value. Now, for the first time in a decade, she felt free. June realized she could finally focus on herself again. She wanted to create a life where she valued herself and her gifts, time, and dreams. Her husband's affair was the turning point. Through this transformative moment, June began building a life that allowed for her to truly feel alive again.

LET GO AND LET GOD

After experiencing turning points, you might look back and realize other signs that you failed to notice had been appearing. Physical sensations, feelings, and signs are always there, but we often ignore them. You might feel a knot in your stomach or ache in your heart. You may be drawn toward something but dismiss it. A certain word or symbol might repeatedly appear for you.

When you decide to make a choice based on a sign, you will discover that life moves in the direction of your energy. When you "let go and let God," all manner of things fall into place. As the shifts begin, keep taking steps toward change, knowing the challenges and chaos will settle into calm and contentment.

Turning points are a time for careful introspection. They allow for a conscious pause. They prepare a time for you to stop, evaluate, and reflect. They present an opportunity for innovative ideas that lead you to necessary changes. As the death of one experience ensues, know that the birth of another is in process. Each of these experiences will be filled with the right and perfect signs to guide your way.

THE INVITATION

Regardless of what is appearing in your world, the universe is attempting to get your attention. It is continually tapping you on the shoulder, whispering in your ear, or sounding a megaphone. Life is speaking with you. What you will come to realize is that you are always on "life support."

Herein is your invitation to uncover the cosmic guidance that is available to you. Something mystical rests beyond the veils of your current understanding. More people in the world are awakening to the magic all around us. Life is interactive. The gateway between the material and mystical is you. Your presence and awareness provide the bridge. It is time to awaken to a brand new experience of you.

Your world is speaking to you. The universe has your back and is guiding your way forward. The information and stories shared here present an opportunity to awaken into a new perspective of the world that surrounds you and clues about how you can move forward while operating within it. Our circumstances and signs may differ, but the wonder and wisdom they inspire resonates equally.

As you awaken to your environment in a more present way, you will see signs. You might not know what they mean at first. Just settle into the joy and delight they bring. As you move forward, you will discover that general meanings exist for all signs, but they also hold deeper, subtler meanings that are specific to you. That is where signs have distinctions. An exciting aspect of "sign" language lies in your discovery of the dialect unique to you.

Every moment of every day holds an invitation, making this seemingly random world an exciting one that is filled with meaning. Even the mundane can hold extraordinary messages. That which seems utterly normal and ordinary might actually hold special symbolism.

THE ORDINARY AS EXTRAORDINARY

W e often take life for granted, especially within our most unconscious, stressful, and bored moments. In challenging times, it might seem unfathomable that Earth is a magical wonderland. However, even ordinary places and experiences court the mystical. Hidden within the ordinariness of life is an extraordinary mystery awaiting your discovery.

In our complex world, everything means something. Your world is speaking to you continuously, but it is up to you to engage in the conversation. In plain sight, amidst daily happenings, the universe has planted unique and special interactions. People, places, and things continually cross your path offering subtle, yet powerful, conversations. As mirrors and reflections, the individuals, items, and experiences you encounter are Divine messengers designed to speak to you, about you.

Whether you will hear the message depends on your open mind and available heart. Consider the wisdom of children. They see things that adults do not. They connect things that the adult mind does not always link. They play with everything in their environment. This is what you are being invited to do with your life.

Play with your relationships, surroundings, and experiences. Look beyond what they represent on the surface. Ask yourself what they bring forward in a more subtle and humorous way. I caution you from keeping your head down. Your seriousness can block your experience of life's lightness. Do not become too focused on daily activities, obligations, work, and struggles, because you might miss the magic that is sitting right in front of you. Be willing to release this conditioning. It was taken on from those who came before you. Awaken to possibility, opportunity, and synchronicity.

Your primary purpose for incarnating is growth, expansion, and the ascension toward your highest potential. You are not alone in this quest but supported in a multitude of ways. You are not abandoned to deal with life on your own. In every step, you will be guided, if you pay attention and stay present. You might be amazed at how life partners with you in reaching your goals, dreams, and desires.

Life's grand design provides messages that support the soul's intention for experiencing form. You came to earth for experience. Mastery over the physical, emotional, and mental aspects of your life is part of that journey. Life will loosen anything that is a barrier to the full breadth and depth of your capability, because expansiveness is the experience your soul desires.

DIVINE DESIGN

Consider the possibility that you invited the ordinary world to play with you. What if your longing for connection and desire for remembrance has activated a cosmic interaction? Is Divine orchestration of communication with the unseen possible? Could this initiation have called forth an emergence of sacred signs?

Your soul designed a default program that is activated whenever you shift from your soul path. You plugged specific signs into certain times and ages to catalyze greater insight and empower particular directions. With this idea in mind, is it possible that life knows where you are to go? A Divine design will continually weave you between your inner and outer world until they merge in alignment with the highest expression of you. Once you begin realizing that the universe is always communicating, you can consciously choose to remain open, curious, and receptive.

Universal intelligence loves you unconditionally. It communicates through signs, symbols, synchronicity, and serendipity. These experiences can appear in a variety of ways and tend to show up when you need a shift in consciousness, need to implement a new behavior, or need to take a new action.

Signs and symbols serve your journey in incredibly powerful ways. They are always reflective, meaning they mirror in equal measure to the degree that they guide. Embrace the sacred encounters you have already met and the ones to come. Remember, they might be hiding within the ordinary... within the extraordinary... and amidst everything in-between.

WHETHER OR WEATHER

Whether you believe or not doesn't matter. Utilizing the philosophy of signs can only help you be a happier person. This is one of the greatest personal growth practices you can undertake. When I began my spiritual and growth path, this was my primary practice. I listened to no teachers, did not embark on trainings, and followed no gurus. I believed that everything I required to grow was inside of me or would be reflected outside of me as the next best step for healing and inquiry. That path has served me very well. Why wouldn't Divine intelligence equip you and your world with everything you require to return home?

Seeing beyond the illusion of inherited beliefs awakens intuitive receptivity and personal power. With a broader vision of reality, the heart opens to its co-creative capacity. There is a great deal more to the world than what your physical eyes perceive. Signs will appear as numbers, insects, animals, words, and anything animate or inanimate. Your body, home, and car also hold innumerable conversations that will appear when most needed. Signs can indicate choices you have made in the past, and they also might empower you to make new choices regarding self-care, self-awareness, and self-empowerment. You hold a Divine design. Anything opposing that design must be dissolved so that your light fully shines.

What if you lived as if everything were a sign intended specifically for you? Every single day begins with a sign that most people take for granted. Sunrise is a sign that reflects your innate brilliance, warmth, and illumination. It is also a sign to wake up! The sun asks you to rise and reach toward an overarching viewpoint; to witness from high above. The sun teaches you to express light and then shine that upon the world. It also guides you to have a consistent rhythm. The sun models how to rise, rest, and retreat. It allows darkness to have a place, so that shadows can be seen.

In the same way, consider the cloudy and rainy days. What if those are signs for you to pause and feel the inside places where you are cloudy? Clouds mirror the heaviness that collects for release. They provide a mirror to give needed space for expressing sadness, grief, and cleansing. Lightning can remind us to tap into anger. Depending on your intuitive guidance, lightning can also mean it is time to strike on an idea. Human nature can be organically expressed using the signs and symbols that nature provides.

The universe utilizes every avenue to get your attention. It wants to play and co-create with you. But a conversation requires at least two; the universe and you. When you encounter a sign, you must respond. You might take an inspired action. Or the sign might be asking you to take the time to dream or journal. Answer the call. The universe is, and has always been, talking to You. How divine that you can access an interactive experience with your soul... with life... and with your source!

SIGNS ARE EVERYWHERE

*W*e live in a world where signs and symbols have been woven into every aspect of our lives. We use signage to communicate with one another. Social conditioning teaches us what some everyday signs mean. As you gained an understanding of how signs offer direction, identity, and connection.... you began using them to navigate the world. You were taught that life's everyday signage served as guideposts for what action to take, how to behave, and which direction to move.

Today, logos, symbols, and insignias appear everywhere, from tattoos to businesses to sports teams. They depict meaning and translate a feeling, brand, or call to action. Some signs—stop signs, one-way signs, and green lights—tell us exactly what to do in traffic. Other signs identify places where we can buy or do specific things. Some signs indicate identity through addresses, street names, and license plates, or company icons, team symbols, and flags.

For thousands of years, signs and symbols have been part of our language. Cavemen used symbols to record their experiences. Ancient Greeks and Romans created signs for the purpose of communication and education. Indigenous people have long utilized natural signs to recognize approaching changes, weather, cataclysms, or messages from Great Spirit. Native Americans are known for using natural objects such as stones and feathers as signs for guidance, direction, and communication.

Literal, practical, and cultural signs not only serve logistically, but also prepare us with nonverbal language mechanics. Now, when encountering subtle and mystical signs, you are already conditioned to respond and follow direction. They created a bridge for grounding the mystical inside of the physical as you discover the world in new ways. But more subtle signs are also available to you for spiritual guidance. A shift in your perspective can help you return to your innate ability to decipher signs of spiritual guidance from the universe.

Life's subtle signs are provided in a constant stream. You might have already noticed some but dismissed them as coincidence or called them synchronicity. These points of awareness came into your life as glimpses, gifts, and direct knowing. Once you recognize what they are, you might realize you've felt their gentle tapping for a while.

Knowingly or unknowingly, you have asked for signs through your questions, pleas, prayers, wishes, or longings. The human desire for experience, connection, and confirmation also brings them about. In fine-tuning the asking, your awareness of signs will expand. By honing receivership, the frequency of your signs will increase.

When you witness how life unfolds on your behalf, that magic will deepen your experience of the mystical. Your actions have been talking to the universe all along. But have you been listening for the answers? In all ways? On all levels?

EARTHLY SIGNS

Signs open you to the fascinating world of symbolism that is embedded within every area of life. Have you ever been driving and spotted a billboard that answered a question you were thinking about? Has a song ever come on the radio that told you exactly what you needed to hear? Have you ever come across a card, quote, or book related to what you were contemplating? Have your eyes ever landed on something specific to what you were feeling? Or you might have found yourself gravitating toward a certain color repeatedly, or a particular number appears for you everywhere you go!

Signs are tangible and intangible; material and immaterial. Within your environment, the signs that help you begin your conversation with the universe might appear as any and everything, including animate and inanimate objects. They encompass the living, such as people, animals, insects, and flowers. They are also material, such as books, cards, artwork, billboards, and other objects. Signs can come through expressions such as songs, smells, and dreams. Sometimes, a sign can be a complete message. This includes things happening within your body, car, home, children, or pets.

NUMBERS

My personal discovery of the expansive world of signs began with numbers. I have had experiences with 11:11 that are simply magical. The number 11:11 on a clock symbolizes a gateway between the physical and spiritual... illusion and reality... mind and heart... and the journey from human "doing" to human "being." Each 1 is symbolic of the pillars of personal mastery that we all must align: physical, mental, emotional, and spiritual. When we see 11:11, a pre-encoded trigger activates within our cellular structure. It is not necessary to know it is there or even believe it. However, science does illustrate that everything in the universe boils down to a binary code of one and zero.

I have experienced communication through numbers for an exceptionally long time. They have continually guided me, telling me exactly when to follow a path, and when to come to a stop. 11:11 has provided reassurance when I was in doubt, and confirmation as I took certain steps. Through these mystical numbers, I began to experience synchronicity.

You might begin seeing 11, 111 or 11:11 as you begin on your soul path, because 11 is a master number. All double-digit numbers are master numbers. As an individual grows in awareness, double digit and triple digit sequences increasingly appear such as 22, 33, 44 or 111, 555, 777. These master number sequences connect to the archangels and ascended masters. They reflect where you are vibrationally. Numbers graduate as you awaken and align to living a more conscious life.

People all over the world see 11:11. If you do not, there is nothing wrong with you. Every person has a unique path and language with the cosmos. If you are seeing *something* repeatedly, you are getting a message. It might be "Take the step that you are considering. The universe will guide you. It has your back," or the message might be, "Not now. Step back and wait." Life is supporting you always.

All numbers have meaning. Whether you are seeing a specific number between one and ten, or a series of repeating numbers that are double, triple, or quadruple digit… each has its own meaning and significance. Numerology is a science of numbers in which multiple-digit sequences are reduced to a single digit. The numerals 1 through 9 have specific meanings that are relevant for understanding the energy of a home or business. These numbers are also used for deciphering an individual's life and soul paths.

All numbers have symbolism and can bring forth incredible insight. If a number is significant, you will see it multiple times. Another way numbers become significant is when your eye lands on a number at a crucial time, and you feel yourself pause. I find it fun to take notice of hotel room numbers when I am traveling. I am enamored by how accurate they always are in their guidance.

The frequency with which numbers appear increases as you continue saying "Yes!" to greater embodiment, inner authority, and authenticity. Whenever numbers appear repeatedly, your question or prayer is being answered. Numbers can be the easiest way to begin understanding how the universe is guiding you.

BOOKS

Have you ever been given a book that offered confirmation for where you are or where you desire to go—like this one? Book titles have always been signs for me. They speak to where I am. Sometimes, if I ask a question of the universe, I'll find a book in my hands that speaks to exactly the issue I am concerned with. Notice the latest books you have read. They will tell a story through their titles and themes, offering another way for you to receive guidance, confirmation, or direction.

I find the same has been true for movies or television shows I am drawn to. I will clarify by saying, it's important to use your conscious intuition rather than passively noticing whatever appears before you on the screen. Conscious choices create a focused dialogue.

MUSIC

Have you ever walked into a store and heard a song that speaks directly to you? The lyrics seem to express what you are thinking or feeling, especially an emotion that needs release in the moment. Think back on what occurred inside of you when this happened. Somewhere within, you experienced a connection beyond words. The moment brought through an experience of stillness that was other-worldly and you felt your heart open because of it. You might have also experienced your mind begin racing with questions due to the synchronicity. The timing of the songs that turn up in our lives can be uncanny and utterly amazing! Sometimes, when you have asked for guidance, you'll hear the answer in the chorus of a song.

WORDS

Have you had your eye land on one word in a billboard or advertisement? That is a sign! Words have power, especially when your eyes randomly find one that strikes a chord. It can be a word in a book or one that appears on your computer screen.

> Years ago, I decided to open a coaching and wellness retreat center. I wanted to name it something beautiful and powerful but could not settle on anything. I asked the universe for guidance. Soon after, I received a card that had the word believe on the cover. Later that day, a song came on the radio; it was titled Believe. The next day, a friend brought a gift. It was a frame that had Believe written across the bottom. And it happened one more time.
>
> That night, digging through a box, I came across a wellness journal that I had written in a couple of years earlier. Within it I had described a vision of a wellness retreat space that would create transformation. The cover of the journal had a butterfly emerging from a cocoon that was hanging off

the "E" in the word Believe, which was also on the cover in cursive writing. I knew I had received my answer.

Our personal names are another type of word guidance. All names have meanings. I believe we are given the name that our soul desires for us to embody. By knowing the meaning of your name, you gain an understanding of who you truly are, and you can begin embodying that. This sign serves as a pathway and return to remembrance.

ANIMALS

Have you ever experienced a hawk fly over when considering a new vision? Has a kitten appeared at your door during a painful time of your life? Was this a time where you needed more unconditional love? Have you experienced a bird, butterfly, or ladybug appear and spontaneously thought of a loved one? Were you surrounded by a swarm of bees during a time you were continually busy with too many things? Did ants appear in your home to tell you it was time to get busy? Animals are wonderful signs. Whether they appear in person or not, they are bringing a message. An animal message can also come through a sticker, postcard, or figurine. I have had animal signs appear via fax.

When you see the same animal repeatedly, it can be considered a totem. Animals and animal totems represent the qualities, characteristics, and expressions of your nature that can be cultivated or that you need to express more fully. Animals mirror your spirit power.

Take special note when unique animals appear on your path. If you see an alligator, a polar bear, or an elephant, it is saying something you need to hear. The universe listens and watches for what you need—and that is why that rhino, flamingo, or whale crossed your path. Receiving a stamp or an animal on an album cover is the same as seeing one walking down the street.

You can also call upon animal spirits, inviting their energies into your life. The same is true for birds, insects, and water creatures. Every creature carries great symbolism. Along with the internet, there are books, card decks, and resources that provide explanations regarding animal symbolism. The Common Sentience book on *Animals* by Steven Farmer details some of these, along with practices for more deeply connecting with your animal totems.

NATURE

Do you have a favorite tree? Have you ever considered what that tree represents for you? Each species of tree has its own meaning and significance. Throughout religious history, trees and their attributes have been used as symbols to portray spiritual truths. Trees have long been revered as ancestors, ancients, and grandmothers or grandfathers. They can be important messengers in a world where there are great divisions and challenges for mankind. Trees are universally appreciated and loved, and therefore celebrated for the signs they provide.

Trees offer healing energy, in addition to powerful wisdom. They have always inspired and offered guidance to those facing big lessons in life. Trees model how humans can live, grow, transition, change, and die with grace. When I look at trees, they remind me to rise high, spread wide, dig deep roots, and shake things off. They also remind me that the interconnectedness of life exists both above and beneath the surface.

Flowers fall into the same category as trees when it comes to the power of symbolism. The various species of flowers offer varied insights and spiritual meanings. In addition, they induce subtle, intuitive guidance through their scents and petal configuration. Fragrance is a powerful and healing component of flowers. Color is another component that provides layered symbolism and energetic healing.

Minerals and crystals are another aspect of nature that possess an entire culture of energetic and healing qualities, even beyond the meaning they bring. While crystals are known for their radiance and beauty, they are also revered for their capacity for spiritual connection. Sacred geometry is another aspect of crystals that taps into cellular memory. Different crystal meanings have been uncovered over the centuries as ancient cultures connected with gems, rocks, and minerals for use in their everyday lives. When a crystal ends up in your hands as a gift, or you find yourself drawn to one, rest assured that the cosmos is giving you exactly the message that is needed. Commune with the crystal. Meditate with it. Keep it in your pocket and let it continue to speak to you.

You will find resources online, in books, and through card decks that offer guidance regarding trees, flowers, leaves, minerals and crystals. Within the Common Sentience series, *Nature* by Ana Maria Vasquez delves into Divine experiences with trees, plants, stones, and landscapes.

LOVE'S SIGNATURE

The universe is filled with a multitude of signs, each laced with the Divine imprint of totality and each expressing a unique soul signature. Every sign is a representation of love and holds this essence, which is built into the life force of everything in our world. It might symbolize love you believe was left behind. When you came to Earth School, you lost yourself. You gave yourself away, forgetting who and what you are. Signs and symbols are a return path to love.

Things that do not feel good to you, are also you. Why? Because love first creates everything unlike itself as a means of reconnecting to itself. Signs of resistance are pieces and parts of you coming forward to be reclaimed, transmuted, and reintegrated. Creation provides incredibly beautiful diversity within the expressions it mirrors to you. This is how you shape-shift before realizing your power and ability to shape-shift. There is no greater interactive, experiential laboratory than Earth School. You are the test subject, the experiment, and the scientist. You are the science within spirituality. You are the signature of love that is embedded within all of it.

Every step made through following your signs is an act of self-love. This interconnection with life builds your beautiful tapestry of creative capacity. This journey is how source experiences your soul signature. Engage in the dance of creation and experience your unique, soulful harmony. What you have been seeking is also seeking you. This is sacred communion and the intimate connection to something you have believed is far beyond reach. But it is not. It is well within your grasp.

As you begin intuiting connections within life, a grid-like matrix will present the complete story of you: your past, present, and future, your generations and lineages. You will see your patterns, behaviors, and inherent talents. When you embrace the freedom and direction of your Divine path, intuiting the necessary steps, this is love in action.

As conversations with the universe unfold more in your life, you will see with new eyes and hear with new ears. In time, you will even taste life in a new way. Experiences will hold more color, becoming clearer and brighter. Signs and symbols will turn up more frequently. Just like a child learning a new language, each day opens a greater degree of fluency.

The time has come for you to open into a beautiful, intimate relationship with the world around you. This will awaken a deeper experience of "internity," while opening you to the possibility of eternity. Continually awaken to the mystery within both realms. Along the way, you will become cognizant of one question softly resounding within your mind:

"Is the universe having a conversation with me?"

Confidently and excitedly, I say, "YES, the universe is having a conversation with you!"

Life sends signs, and each arrives in a uniquely loving way, and in conspiracy for greater good. The universe has a quirky sense of humor, too. Give way to its playful interaction. Engage this adventure without limitation and awaken to Divine direction, and you will begin looking at life as a compass.

LIFE AS A COMPASS

t is natural to wonder if there is more to life, if something larger exists, and whether life is communicating with you. Sometimes, perhaps often, you experience not knowing who you are. You may have no idea where you are going or why you are here. You might feel lost and confused. Moments will appear when there are too many choices, and the right one is unclear. At these moments, signs support you in the greatest way. They become your compass.

Places you traverse may appear unmarked, but they are filled with the signs required for clarity. Life's signs will direct you from the dark night of your soul to the light of each new day. In time, signs will bring you out of worry, helping you alleviate anxiety and stress. Trust that the universe always guides you, and wait for a sign. Simply disconnect your brain, so that the ego does not drive you in every direction. Be open to the signs and follow life's compass.

Whether you choose the expression of stomping, screaming, sobbing, or breaking down—or you opt for begging, praying, calmly asking, or sitting silently—the universe will respond to your call. However, if you fight life, it can be easy to miss what is right in front of you. The surrendered self can more easily land upon the specific sign meant as a guidepost. Regardless of how the moment appears, know that your universal connection has been forged. Cosmic communication is available at every turn.

When you need an answer, one will fall within your purview, sight, scope of listening, or sensorial landscape of feeling. Built into your cellular structure is the ability to tap in, recognize, reconnect, and remember. You are threaded to life. You can never be apart from it, no matter what you might believe. Within each breath is enough movement to orchestrate an entire universe—one which is always at your disposal.

In your surrender—whether to fear, anxiety, the moment, or a higher part of you—life will meet you. Through your five senses, and your sixth, each sign will express something of significance. Awareness is eminent. A frozen moment-in-time will offer you a sense of timelessness and deep connectivity. A knowing will strike as your heart opens. Inspiration will rise. Fear will transform into awe. Where no possibility existed, a tiny opening will appear.

You will relish in seeing, feeling, and sensing the delight of a precisely placed sign. Within that minuscule moment lies the instruction, direction, and prompting for your next, best, most appropriate step. You might not have realized that life has had this built-in guiding compass. Signs are in-your-face—yet sometimes invisible—tools that are always at your disposal.

TRUST

Look back on the moments when you asked for a sign. There might also be occasions when you received a sign but didn't trust it. Perhaps you then asked for more signs, as added confirmation. At some point, you will make the decision to trust your sign, because not trusting will not get you anywhere. Get out of your head and into your heart. Let life lead you in the direction you are designed to go. The greatest benefit of signs is their ability to help you learn to trust. As you learn to follow your signs, you will find yourself trusting the universe... trusting life... and ultimately, trusting yourself.

Up to now, you may have been caught within an illusion of your own making. That sleep state ensnared you, causing you to remain outer-focused. You missed many signs along the way. Within this dual world, it is easy to do. Distraction and busyness can make us too serious and shortsighted, which further distances us from the lighter side of life. Signs are easy to discount when we are distracted. But when we refuse to listen, life must resort to what is close to us. After attempting to leave signs in your workplace, home, and relationships with no response, life may use your body as the conversation-starter.

Most signs initially appeared externally because of how outwardly focused people are. Yet the external is merely guiding us to go within; to come home. Subtle messages might keep appearing. As an added nudge, your insides start tugging. Your body will ache or pain as an indicator that you need to stretch, heal, or shift. All messages arise to lead individuals back to their own center.

You do not need to hunt for signs, just try to notice them. You cannot help but meet them at the right time. The universe provides guidance, advice, and answers for any question you have, however important or miniscule. You don't have to guess. Just pay attention. The shift for your issue, problem, challenge, or circumstance exists within the awareness often catalyzed by a sign that appears. The sign brings forth a perspective different from what you believe now.

Explore what is unfolding by taking your signs inside. Delve into the inner work that is being called for, while also cultivating your powers of intuition. The most essential element of any sign is the feeling it instills within you. Let it direct you into embodying the full experience each turning point elicits.

It is a blessing to awaken to, and become aware of, our interconnection with life. But such blessings must be invited, accepted, and held sacred. The magic involves asking, which invites consciousness to flow within the joy of sacred encounters. Asking for help opens you to knowing more help will be offered.

The more you trust life, and say YES to what is being offered, the greater your capacity to discern communication, wisdom, and understanding. The rewards are immediate and the feeling is unmistakable. The deep peace and joy you will find strengthens an empowering experience of involution, which mirrors the evolutionary upward spiral of your life.

HEAL

Signs will continue coming. If you don't engage with the conversation that is present, you and your life will feel stagnant. If you doubt your connection, the signal will weaken. Make no mistake; the universe remains present. Through confusion and doubt, you may not. When you are in a state of unconscious numbness, the universe's first task is to bring attention to how you are being. Signs will appear to support greater embodiment and presence.

You determine the degree of punctuation required to gain your attention and presence. Life follows your command to deliver the necessary signs. Be sure to initiate punctuation that supports a calm conversation rather than a loudly echoing one. Life presents messages in whatever manner you most need to receive them. Through a variety of expressions, from "boulder-experiences" that stop you in your tracks to "pebble-experiences" that momentarily trip you up, life provides a conversation that is intended for healing.

The universe will begin nudging you awake. Pebbles provide a gentle push. When that does not work, rocks are placed on your path. If this does not move you into action, boulders will appear. Boulders arrive when you refuse to look, listen, or pay attention to more subtle signs. They are the megaphone used to bring attention to what is out of alignment. Do not judge how they appear, or the way the universe is forced to communicate with you. In your slumber, moments for a firm two-by-four might become necessary.

The universe speaks in ways that stretch you beyond your belief systems and self-imposed restriction. The universe constantly places symbols, signs, and dialogue in your path that supports the full recognition of your truth and highest expression. Every aspect of your humanity—your emotions, desires, attachments, and manifestations—holds a clue in a language specific to you. Be the receiver. Answer the calls as they appear. Then lean in and connect to the aspect of you that the universe is calling forth.

Dialogue with the universe becomes more powerful when it is no longer denied. When you consider who you are, what you feel, and what is being reflected, you receive a glimpse of your greater wholeness. As you embrace coincidence, synchronicity, and everyday miracles as worthy and normal experiences, your acceptance signals the YES that means you will continue opening to and strengthening yourself. This engages a more deeply embodied experience of living, being, and knowing.

FEEL

The law of attraction does not bring you signs, symbols, language, lessons, and experiences based only on what you are thinking. This language manifests based on what you are feeling. The mind is merely a computer. It stores, analyzes, and computes. The heart feels, attracts, and creates. The universe is always asking, "What do you feel like today?" Then it sends mirrors of that to you. When you react or respond with feeling—conscious and aware or unconscious and repressed—the universe provides correlating experiences and signs.

Life wants you to consciously embrace every experience. Only then does it not need to repeat circumstances. If similar experiences appear, these only come to deepen your awareness of residual energies within you that might be resisting the message. Subsequent experiences and signs always bring new and unique differences. Life experiences itself in, as, and through you, repeatedly.

Do not avoid or attempt to escape any of your experiences. Fully immerse within them. Stop running away from emotions. Fully feel them. Remain energetically and emotionally present. Do not suppress your emotions. Fully integrate them. Growth and change occur through the natural and organic path of feeling everything fully. To connect more deeply to signs, cultivate your ability to be with your feelings. To expand your dialogue and dialect, place all inquiries within your heart and immerse into what is brought forward.

Because of free will and choice, you are presented with signs and experiences that might seem ambiguous. This allows you to determine the next step. It is in your power to create the reality of your choosing. It is not that you live in a world of duality. Instead, your perceptions are of a dual nature, thus creating an experience of duality. You are the creator and co-creator. It is for you to choose how to look at every experience, sign, and expression.

Initially, some signs and experiences might trigger you, resulting in a greater experience of duality. This can have you reacting from judgment, blame, or distress. If that occurs, the opportunity to discover patterns held by your wounded self is available. In this case, the first step is to feel and know the unknown parts of you.

If you have been numb, feelings will become activated. In this case anger, blame, and shame are higher than numbness. In witnessing your own reactions, you can make different choices. As you become more conscious, your level of reactivity will lessen. You will access higher levels of emotional intelligence. As you do, the shift from reactivity to response builds. This change will reflect in your experiences and through the signs that start appearing for you.

Symbols and signs that appear within chaos, challenge, and change are here to remind you to connect to what is real, what is good, and what is true. They appear to help you see the larger landscape instead of the limited perception of the human condition. The topography of humanity is a vast landscape of feeling. Signs, symbols, and synchronous experiences help raise emotional intelligence so that vibratory frequency increases and attracts solutions. Ponder the following questions as a means for increasing your level of emotional intelligence.

1. What feelings regularly rise within you?
2. Which feelings do you avoid, push down, ignore, dislike, and repress?
3. Are you currently being nudged to face and embrace certain feelings?
4. What unacknowledged feelings cause experiences to appear and reappear?
5. What signs are pointing to feeling more deeply?
6. What is required for you to feel fully?
7. Can you allow the feelings to rise and simply be with them?

Embrace life's incredible array of signs so that what no longer serves you flows out of your experience. Do not allow any emotion to sit and fester. Do not let your container become stagnant and cloudy with suppressed emotion. Allow cyclical moments of emptiness. Create space. Fill and empty repeatedly, so that awareness anchors your natural rhythm. Do not view emptiness as a need to refill too quickly and rush back into fullness.

Space and vacancy refine and recalibrate the evolutionary process so that you open to the ebb and flow of life, signs, and expansion. Continually replenish with joyful experiences. Be the essence of both spectrums, the inner and outer. You are all of it. You are sacred space, the holding of space, and space surrounding all things.

SIGNS EMPOWER INTUITION, CONNECTION, AND FREEDOM

————— • ◉ ◉ ◉ • —————•

*M*ost caregivers do not present the mystical and magical to young children, nor do they explain how to cull the extraordinary from within the ordinary. No institution or social construct teaches children where to look, what to look for, or how to interpret what is found. The hidden language of signs is not taught in schools, brought up in business meetings, or usually mentioned in dinner conversation. Signs rest in the realm of the unspoken, which is why they remain unseen for as long as they do.

Within the deep recesses of your mind, you may wonder what is happening. Whether it is a cloud expressing a face or image, a tree that seems to reach toward you, a mountain depicting strength, an animal bringing gifts, the weather modeling your emotion, or experiences playing out your deepest behaviors . . . the universe is speaking! You are safe. You are protected. You are Divine.

Through increased conscious presence, you can expand this ongoing dialogue. What initially begins as pathways of awareness will soon become turning points in life and Divine guideposts for increased devotion for the journey of your soul.

EMPOWERING INTUITION

None of this is going to seem logical when you start out. It might even seem outright crazy. The people around you are not likely to understand. Yet, at some point, you will find that life could be no other way, nor would you want it to be. Commit to awakening to what is naturally around you. As your life begins changing for the better, naysayers are going to want "what you've got." There is something very real happening, and it is far beyond anything practical or logical.

Your first steps require trust. You must trust that your messages will come because you are willing to show up. Trust that you have not lost your mind. Trust that you are valuable enough to receive from the universe. This means trusting "self" and the intuitive capacity that develops, even if others in your life don't play along. Trust your newly arising spirit-vision.

Strengthening intuition and rediscovering the secret language of the cosmos reunites you with a forgotten part of yourself. Intuition touches the eternal within. Keep going deeper. Ask the essential questions. Open to the clues that the universe provides. Piece together the puzzle of your life. Each time you do this, your sixth sense is empowered.

The appearance of signs and symbols is important, but it is not the end goal. The feelings they prompt and how they direct your thoughts is of greater significance. All of life is in collaboration with you for a greater experience of self-awareness. Symbolism and synchronicity flirt with you through a courtship between the physical and spiritual. When you take notice of the mystical, more questions will arise. This is a means of expansion. With it, eventually more answers will come.

In the beginning, you might want to conduct extensive research to understand what a sign is telling you. It is normal to look everywhere to find answers. Eventually, research will no longer be necessary. Your intuition will become increasingly powerful. You will begin to intuit meanings that are unique to you. This will expand into a dialect that is specific for you. Each person has their own language with the universe. In becoming comfortable with how signs appear, you will develop a deepened understanding, beyond what you are learning in this book. Cultivate intuitive prowess. Be open to playing.

You may think signs mean the same thing for every person. In general terms, they will. However, your signs are designed for you. They fit your unique perceptions, feelings, and desires. Another person might experience the same sign, in the same moment, but derive a completely different meaning. In other cases, you might see something that means a great deal to you, whereas the person with you will have no connection to it at all. You are both correct.

Your conversations will attune to your viewpoint. You will also begin to understand the conversations others are having with the universe, even if they cannot. A continual "YES" maintains this cosmic dialogue as an exciting, intuitive interaction. What you discover has spanned throughout time, often going unheard and unnoticed. As opposed to lucid dreaming, this is lucid waking. Are you listening? Will you answer the call? Will you say "YES" again, and again, and . . . again?

DÉJA VU

Have you ever walked into a place and felt you had been there before? Maybe you have been in a conversation, and you recall already having had that dialogue before. Some déjà vu experiences occur in real life. Others appear in dream time and are then followed by the real life experience. Either way, this glitch is symbolic of timelessness, oneness, and awakening. You are experiencing confirmation of your eternity, by reliving something that has not yet occurred or foreseeing something that has already happened. Déjà vu means "already seen." It is a unique sign of heightened intuition.

REPETITION

Do you experience repeating patterns? Do certain experiences occur over and over? Do you see the same word, bird, or number repeatedly? Do you injure yourself in the same place repeatedly? If something happens repeatedly, this is a sign from the universe that holds a deeper meaning. It can also mean you are not paying attention, so the universe is going to great lengths to provide something recognizable.

The human brain recognizes patterns and repetition. Due to prior conditioning of literal signage and other memorized matter, the brain looks for connections through patterns. The subconscious mind utilizes this mechanism for linking the seen and the unseen. Intuition deciphers meaning from repeating visual stimuli and corresponding elements. Self-awareness brings the subconscious world to the surface with intuitive awareness. The repetition of signs is a gentle tapping, or knocking, to get your attention and encourage greater awareness and personal growth.

If you find certain things repeating, make note of them. Often, you are being directed to perceive something subtle but significant. Take the time to inquire, contemplate, and feel into the experience. Reflect on what you have asked for and see how this repetition might be attempting to guide you in that direction.

SYNCHRONICITY

Have you ever been thinking of a person, and they call you? Have you ever needed to contact someone, and you bump into them? There are certain magical moments when it feels as if the stars align, and everything comes together. It could be the perfect meeting of two individuals. Have you experienced having an issue, and then someone with a solution appears?

Synchronicity is a sign of alignment. These moments occur when you are present, aligned, and living in right time. Incidents align within your individual experience that defy the laws of probability and are far outside any rational sequence of events. These types of serendipities mirror your inner world. Synchronicity means you are on the right path. It can also indicate that your answer, solution, or need is on the way.

INSPIRING CONNECTION

Self longs to find itself in the brightness of the star, the innocence of a baby, and in the flight of a butterfly. Self desires to flow as abundantly as a waterfall, strike like lightning, blow through the trees, and reach the high peak of the tallest mountain. How do you know these things are you? They feel good to you. They bring you happiness and joy. You can only recognize that which you are!

These are not coincidences, a blur of vision, or something that you need to second-guess. Simply open your mind and consider expanding into them. Let your body tell you what the sign makes you feel. Let your heart speak to you before allowing mind chatter to distract you.

Spirit also exists within duality. The universe uses every available avenue to support you. As the journey unfolds, messages will appear in the exact guise of what you need to see and hear. Beauty exists inside the dual world as well. Everything supports celebrating all that you are, light and dark. Open to every mirror, each reflection, and all the signs, regardless of how they appear. When you receive signs that send your mind spinning into fear, remember that there truly is no "bad" sign. Even signs that appear ominous have positive aspects and golden doorways. Confusion and chaos are engaged by choice. You always have the choice of moving to higher ground.

It is easy to find yourself in things you have been conditioned to see as "good." Become equally aware of which things you have been taught to view as negative or "bad." Your viewpoint affects how you perceive a sign. Surrender to what is natural and holy about everything. Everything is you. All of life is Divine. Each moment is a turning point toward a new level of consciousness. In becoming more aware, you will see that symbols and signs lead in this direction. The universe is always loving and generous.

The intelligence of the universe is boundless. It is always connected to you and desires to strengthen its connection with you. It is up to you to cultivate a real desire to converse with the universe. Be steadfast. You must be willing to receive the communications no matter how they show up, or from whom they come. Answers can come from any source: a billboard, an experience, or a random person. The possibilities for communication are endless. You may not always realize this, particularly if you're going through struggle, challenge, or chaos.

As sign conversations weave into each life circumstance, touching you uniquely, they can be heard as whispers resting deep inside. Your job is to raise the whisper's volume so that the conversation is brought to life, and into the light. Your soul is calling for you to lean into a conversation of higher guidance. When the universe is speaking, you need only respond with a "YES!"

Some signs will cause you to pause; to quietly ponder. Others will create inner and outer stillness, even if only for a few seconds. Sometimes, they will send you in a tizzy so that you witness your own insanity. With all of these, you will reach a moment where you experience presence and awareness. If fortunate, you will hold on to this for a time, before being whisked back into distraction. A deeper part knows that you are more than you believe yourself to be. You are more than your identity, personality, mind, body, or soul. This is the mystery.

DREAMS

Do you dream? Are your dreams vivid? Do they sometimes seem bizarre? If you're open to receiving messages from the universe through your dreams, keep a dream journal close to your bed. Signs can appear within your dreams.

Dreaming is a wonderful avenue for guidance. It often supplies solutions from the subconscious and higher self. The subconscious represents all the information that the conscious mind cannot access. However, because it is rooted in the vastness of the universe, messages can arise through the dream state. You access higher wisdom when you sleep.

Utilize a dream journal to keep track of significant signs or messages. If you can remember details, record them. Colors, words, numbers, animals, and objects are all signs within a dream that provide guidance. Anything and everything in a dream is a sacred offering for guidance.

SENSATIONS

Do you experience twinges, aches, goosebumps, or tingles? Odd sensations in the body are pointers. These signs can illustrate areas that require introspection. They can also depict premonitions or positive ideas. Many times, twinges and aches relate to things that are suppressed. Sometimes, these are warnings.

Emotions and feelings are signposts that help you navigate life. Sometimes your feelings of fear or anxiety are trying to protect you. You are being guided to use caution, particularly if you feel emotions that seem out of place.

Gut feelings are your intuition having a clear sense of knowing. Gut feelings are the intelligence of the unconscious.

Other types of signs appearing as sensations relate to disease or discomfort. These signs might turn up as health symptoms or issues. Every part of the body means something. Different areas of the body connect to certain emotions or to masculine and feminine energies. Things on the front side of the body concern the future. Issues affecting the back of the body relate to the past. Your physical vessel is an incredible arena for messages.

OLFACTORY STIMULATION

Have you ever experienced a scent or smell that took you to another time or place? Have you ever smelled roses when no roses were in sight? The universe may be using olfactory stimulation to connect you to something that is relevant to a current experience. Scent is often a way that angels bring signs. You can discover more about angel communication in the Common Sentience book *Angels* by Tricia McCannon.

Some smells evoke vivid memories, triggering either positive memories and uplifting emotions, or incidents of wounding and trauma. Your sense of smell can detect scents that are relevant to your present inquiry or challenge.

EXPANDING FREEDOM

Ultimately, every individual is attempting to make sense of life, so that their life holds meaning. The desire for proof of connection and purpose threads through our interactions, experiences, and encounters. Mind wants to identify what and why. It likes to wrap explanations around things, attaching perceptions that eventually become the stories told repeatedly. These then become embedded beliefs that can limit and bind us from knowing the vast truth of who we really are.

When life has no meaningful purpose, we know that something is lacking. This might prompt us to begin seeking. It is the moment that we plead, "Please, send me a sign." This plea is the permission the universe requires to show us that there is more to the world than we once believed.

Whenever you allow yourself to feel innocence and childlike wonder—even during times of anxiety, stress, or skepticism—you leap from the edge of illusion to land safely on something more real. In the next moment, a sign will blaze brightly in front of you. Catch it. Do not miss it. The sign will light up and seem bigger than everything else around it.

Enlist experiences that catalyze your adventure of a lifetime. Through this lens, dive deeply into what life is offering, explore what appears, and eagerly move toward wherever you feel led. Listen for the hints and clues that life offers. Unlock your heart. Life is meant to feel good. Each sign and symbol is leading you to that feeling. Receive your childlike innocence and playfulness. Experience the lover's joy and live in expectancy of hearing from your beloved.

MANIFESTATION

Are you delighted by manifestations, especially when something you genuinely want appears out of nowhere? Do you always get the perfect parking spot? Do you receive free items?

Sometimes money appears. A friend brings a gift. You end up with a duplicate shipment and the merchant tells you to keep it. With greater alignment and expectancy, life creates receptivity. Manifestation is a symbol of how abundant you feel. Each manifestation will also have its own distinct meaning. When you are encountering repeated blessings, the universe is confirming that you are on track.

PEOPLE

The most interesting messages come through other people. How simply ingenious that you attract signs which reflect what and who you are. The people who get under your skin—trigger, annoy, anger, upset, and push your buttons—are incredible signs. They are the best representations of what you do not want to see about yourself.

People mirror through their behavior and words. This mirroring is a precious gift. It lets you know what beliefs and behaviors of yours need attention. As signs, people illustrate what is held within your inner landscape. This is most often what is unconscious within you.

In the same vein, those that you love, admire, celebrate, enjoy, adore, and are inspired by also reflect who you are. Once again, they illustrate what is repressed within you. The constellation of people that surround you reflect the topography of your multidimensional self.

The universe is one amazingly beautiful thought of continuous creation that longs to reveal itself through each one of us. It uses our personal creations to do so. This is also projected through the signs and symbols of people in your path. Your expansion awaits within everything. Are you willing to notice the mystical quality of your interactions and experiences? The Divine is always appearing in a different place, with another face, to show you more of yourself.

Serendipity, coincidence, omens, and other out-of-the-blue occurrences arise to get your attention. The universe can have a quirky sense of humor. You might not laugh in the moment, but do not be surprised if you find yourself chuckling when you look back. Even in your unconscious moments, the universe is consciously orchestrating life on your behalf.

Initially, when you see straightforward signs, you might chalk them up to being mere coincidence. It is okay to be skeptical. Become an explorer of experience. Let life surprise you. Be open to embracing a new perspective of reality. You might be surprised at how life possesses an abundant ability for radiating flow. At the very least, life will create an opening for the wonderful and whimsical to dance between the real and surreal.

COMMON MISCONCEPTIONS ABOUT SIGNS

———• • ◉ ◉ ◉ • ———•

*W*hat are your first thoughts when you see a black cat cross your path? A crack in the sidewalk? The number 666?

Where does your mind go when you experience a flat tire? What would you think if there were a flood in your basement? Is it possible for experiences such as these to have beneficial meanings? Could they illustrate something entirely different than the negative perspective that most people would have?

Black cats symbolize mystery, mysticism, and magic. Black is the color of potentiality and creation—the void. A flood represents purification. It also symbolizes abundance, or a time of impending overflow. A flat tire indicates a need to rest, slow down, and pause. It is a time to breathe deeply. And 666? This is a positive and auspicious angel number.

If you wonder whether you hold negativity, judgment, or superstition, consider some of the images held within our social mythology. Everyone wants the world to feel safe within their experiences and within the universe. Each sign and awareness support you in grounding into the ever-growing comfort that you are guided and protected. The deeper you venture into your language of connection, the greater sense of courage you will garner.

People often feel timid about openly sharing their sacred encounters. These connections are intimate, it can make us feel vulnerable to tell others about them. We might fear being judged as "weird, woo-woo or crazy." But this is not craziness or make-believe. This is real life.

We all experience signs. A smile, a gasp, and the state of awe inevitably emerges during every synchronous encounter. Signs are part of awakening to more of the self. In becoming more comfortable in your skin, and with an ever-deepening trust in your universal connection, the ability to share these treasured, mystical moments more openly also expands. As you begin sharing, you will become a catalyst for everyone around you to come forward with their spiritual stories.

TECHNOLOGY ISSUES

Have you ever experienced your printer not working? What about your phone? Maybe it was a garage door, or the air conditioning, or you discovered a glitch in your car's computer or electrical system. Technology and electrical issues are all signs from the universe. Any type of breakdown is. Generally, these signs are attempting to stop you, slow you down, or have you at least pause for a bit.

These kinds of things often occur during Mercury retrograde. Do you wonder why? Mercury retrograde is a time for looking back. It is a period when people are advised to reflect and heal. This is what the planet reversing symbolizes. The universe assists by creating technology and communication malfunctions because we should be focusing on our interiors, not the exterior.

Any issue in a car or home has to do with the self. Both represent the physical body. So, next time you have a flat tire, it is likely because you are depleted or heading in that direction. If you have a toilet or plumbing issue at home, it might be that you have blocked emotions that need to be released.

HEALTH ISSUES

All physical issues stem from an emotional and spiritual cause. This means your health issues relate to suppressed emotion, discordant beliefs, and negative energy. Every organ and area of the body relates to a certain emotion. Each area of the body connects to a chakra energy center which correlates to an area of your body and life. Metaphysically, the left side of the body represents the feminine, and the relationship with your childhood female caregiver. The right side represents the masculine, and your relationship to the childhood male caregiver.

The baggage you carry causes your aches, pains, and illness. This is the dust that collects and clogs our systems. Life holds challenges, obstacles, heartbreak, and things that happen for no apparent reason. If you carry those experiences beyond when they occur, you might end up hurt—but they are not hurting you. We hurt ourselves when we carry such weight. There is nothing worth carrying if it negatively impacts your health. Every moment is experience, just experience. Be mindful of how you feel. If you're experiencing pain, ask yourself, what am I carrying that is hurting me? These moments of inquiry hold your aha's, awakening, and insight... if you want to absolutely love yourself into freedom.

DELAYS, COMPLICATIONS, AND CHALLENGES

Have you ever experienced flight delays or cancellations, or complications with an order arriving on time? When something is not meant to be, do not fight it. Life is telling you to let go of control. It is attempting to slow you down so that the Divine plan can catch up with your ego-driven plan. The universe has a plan for you. Sometimes, people are so busy with their own plan that it causes the universe to have to keep redirecting us. Delays and complications are asking you to reconsider your course of action.

SUPERSTITION

Has a black cat ever crossed your path? Would you walk under a ladder? What if a home you were looking at had an address of 666? Superstitions, omens, and bad luck have become part of the folklore and mythology of fear. Ideas passed down through the generations are *belief systems* but they may not be accurate. Whatever you believe to be true will dictate your words, actions, and behaviors. Reconsider what you want to claim as dogma. When considering general ideas of superstition, where does your mind go? To love or to fear?

> Catherine was extremely upset when she reached out to me. The church she grew up in had to change their phone number, due to a company merger. Their new number contained a "666." She did not want "the devil's number" associated with her church. She could not understand why the universe would allow this.

As you consider this scenario, how do you feel? Do you hold the same belief regarding 666? Is this number inappropriate for a church? Are you neutral around it? Is it simply a number? Could there be another way of looking at the situation? What might this sign be calling for Catherine to shift? Out of all the numbers that exist, would the universe actually deem one number as unworthy, demonic, or bad?

The idea of 666 being connected to the devil is a myth that was propagated by the movie industry, stories, and fear. In truth, anything can be "of the devil" if someone suggests it and others believe it. Actually, 666 is a beautiful angel number. It is ideal for a church. In angelic hierarchy, seraphim have six wings and communicate with humans clairvoyantly, through our sixth sense. The number six is the symbol of balance and special powers unique to the angelic realm.

When you see the number 666, it is a sign to focus on personal spirituality to balance and heal any life issues. Be open to receiving help, love, and support from all realms, human and angelic. Therefore, 666 is a perfect sign for people seeking religious and spiritual guidance.

Anything can be made "bad," but how does that serve higher consciousness? Check in with yourself regarding the superstitions you carry. Be discerning in how you allow fear to perpetuate ignorance and empower its own consciousness. What we each hold carries great power in creating our world. How could the Divine have created anything that does not carry the highest vibrations of love, when everything is embodied with Divine energy?

Signs support you in questioning beliefs, so that you expand your level of consciousness. As you grow in higher consciousness, it is important to realize that the power of your frequency also contributes to co-creating our world. As a light worker, you contribute more powerfully than an unconscious individual. Because of your greater level of awareness, any thought you hold will be more powerful. What you believe impacts the world you live in.

PROJECTION

Belief and projections of something being "bad" is a perspective of distrust in the universe, and of the Divine plan. Judgment can keep signs from being received. When judging anything, separation is created. In truth, what appears as separation externally is really an illustration of your separation that exists internally. Your judgment of anyone or anything illustrates where you are disconnected and judging yourself. Become aware of how you see, perceive, and judge your environment. This will open a completely new conversation with the universe, which is an entirely different expanse of signs.

Step away from projections taken on through your conditioning and experiences. Do not project hardship, negativity, or toxicity onto the experiences, signs, or symbols that appear. With a slower pace, breathe in what is around you. Respond rather than react. Open your eyes and mind to what you would not otherwise see. Recline into each moment so that you immerse within the experience and lift it to higher ground. Breathe.

Enter each experience as if you are brand new, born again, and innocent. Inhale the wonder of everything that appears upon your path and cultivate a neutral mind. Cast no judgment. Simply witness and strive to find neutrality in all things.

KEEP IT SIMPLE

Do you tend to complicate things? Are you too serious? Have you forgotten how to play? A key touchstone of the universe is simplicity. It will not waste energy. Allow signs to be what they initially represent for you. Do not overcomplicate them with analyzing, second-guessing, or demanding additional confirmations.

You may get lost while on your journey. This might happen many times over. You could venture down a path that is opposite of the sign, because your ego takes over. You might get in your own way. Even if this occurs, keep things simple by fully engaging the experience you are in. The universe knows how to use where you are to take you to where you most desire to be.

THE POWER OF INNOCENCE

From a neutral space, without the judgments of good or bad, allow yourself to discover the opportunities that a consciousness of innocence brings forth. Life is continually beckoning you into higher conversation. Within every landscape—inner, outer, and with the universe—signs ask you to approach life and your experiences innocently. Your work is to reclaim your natural rhythm and engage with the world from a pure place. In each moment that you open your heart and choose love, your experience transforms. Become part of the greater conversation—as the universe—in active dialogue with everything.

The language of symbolism resonates with the truth of the soul. Of course, it can be colored when you use your mind to figure things out. By moving with wonder and embodying a heart of childlike openness, clarity reveals itself and guides you toward truth. Innocence invites more magic and play into your experience.

The conscious commitment to being Spirit in human form is a huge leap from the general consciousness of our world. People intellectualize this, but integration is a completely different level of expansion. Not every person reaches this "YES." Such consciousness fully acknowledges, accepts, and celebrates the connection to all things as a part of the one great Self.

You require no special anointing to know your connection in, as, and with Spirit. It simply requires asking, allowing, and receiving. Set your beliefs aside. Be a scientist and spiritualist. Explore life's treasure map as it appears. There is nothing to fear. You are always loved, guided, and protected. Only good exists within the universe. It can be no other way.

Notice what you are introduced to. In each moment, see how this plays out to form a melody. Attune to your soul song, which plays without you having to know its sound. Your soul melody is as natural and organic as intuitive guidance. Touch the perfect beauty and magic of this new world. In allowing life's signs to guide your steps, a greater harmony will unfold. You will feel your soulful rhythm each day.

Open to the beauty that links everything. Breathe deeply, and take in the mystery, the magic and the mystical. Let each of these stories inspire remembrance of signs you may have encountered before, and curiosity about those signs yet to come.

PART TWO

Sacred Encounters with Pathways,
Turning Points, and Divine Guideposts

The wisest men follow their own direction and listen to no prophet guiding them. None but the fools believe in oracles, forsaking their own judgment.

— EURIPIDES

TIME TO WAKE UP

*T*he "elevens" started turning up at one of the lowest moments of my life. Just when I thought I couldn't handle seeing another special number, it hit me: I needed to ask the universe to explain the message. The answer was a future I would not have believed.

I stepped into my prayer room after a rough night with little sleep, feeling traumatized and numb. I could not seem to pray this morning. Every cell inside me wanted to scream instead. I could not understand why life held so much pain.

Before long, I was on my knees and in tears.

I had been sternly told as a young child that I should never cry, or "God will make you cry." So, I learned to be strong for so long, holding back tears all my life—and now, in my late thirties, the dam was finally breaking.

Once I began to cry, the tears flowed relentlessly. I experienced a long overdue, enormous release.

My legs would no longer allow me to stand in defiance of my circumstances. I became a heap, a convulsing and crying mess on the floor. I pleaded through the tears, until my words became a soft whisper: "Help me.

Help me. Help me . . . Please, send me a sign... something... anything... Let me know I am not alone...that I can find a way out."

I simply wanted the pain to end. I wanted to truly live—or I would rather die. I wanted no more of whatever "this" was. I had suffered for so many years that I could not imagine facing any more pain than I had already experienced. My body was clinging to this pain.

Then, I disappeared.

I surrendered to some deep place inside—somewhere between here, there, and nowhere. For a while, I no longer was. I had no thoughts, no feelings, no time, and no form. I left my body and my awareness traveled elsewhere. Only silence and space remained.

I was still on the floor when my awareness returned. Unsure of how long I had been lying there, I attempted to gather myself, but this new experience had stunned me. I was someone who was always in control. During this experience, there was no control. There was... nothing. A gentle realization momentarily surfaced that, "If I did not exist, neither did the pain."

I had been sprawled across my prayer room floor long enough for dusk to become dawn. Had one day, two, or more gone by? I began breathing deeply, so that I could regain control of myself. What had happened?

The hallway clock ticked rhythmically. To ground myself, I focused on its loud, consistent sound. The room felt strangely warm. My skin was extra sensitive. It was as if all my senses had sharpened.

I became aware of the sun cascading upon me; just me. It did not shine anywhere else in the room, as if this beautiful light was holding me. A thought flashed quickly through my mind: *What if this is a sign that "my dark night" is over and light is finally dawning?*

I brushed the silly thought away, muttering, "It would be nice to receive a message. I sure could use a few."

Then, out of complete frustration, I declared loudly, "You are welcome to talk to me anytime. I am waiting . . ."

The room was silent.

My comment sounded ridiculous. What was I thinking? It wasn't like a booming voice was going to speak from overhead. After praying so many years for peace, I was no longer sure that anyone was listening.

I stood. I had no idea what time it was, but I knew I needed to get on with the day. Before exiting the room, I glanced at the clock sitting in the corner: 11:11. Goosebumps covered my arms. My body shivered, even though I was not cold. The sensations made me pause, but for only a second.

I had no idea that my request had just sparked something. I had given myself permission to connect with a conversation that had been present all along. Not until years later I would discover this dialogue had always been happening. However, in the early portion of my life, I had been too distracted to notice and not present enough to receive it.

The next day, the phone rang. The caller said, "Answer the call"—and then, they hung up. *Strange!* For some reason, my mind returned to the 11:11 I'd seen the previous day. I was perplexed. My eyes landed on the microwave's clock as I turned to put the phone down: 11:11. Why was I seeing this again? I quickly dismissed the thought, grabbed my keys, and proceeded toward the garage. I had errands to run.

As I reached the end of the driveway and paused to look both ways, I noticed a big commotion in the lot across the street, which was being cleared for another home. A bulldozer pushed dirt to one side, creating a long drive. As it turned so the side of the vehicle faced me, I saw "1111" painted across the equipment's side! I rubbed my eyes to be sure I was seeing correctly. *How weird.*

I remained confused as I set about my errands until finally, I had one last stop: the grocery store. As I turned into the parking lot, I noticed the mileage on my car: 11011. *Another coincidence.* Once inside the store, I quickly gathered what was needed. The cashier in the checkout line was chatty. I tried to be interested, but my mind drifted to the coincidences of the day. I wondered, *What is happening? Am I losing my mind?*

The cashier paused her endless chatter and expressed a squeal of delight. "Your total is $111.11. That's cool!" The freckle-faced young lady popped her chewing gum as she smiled at me.

Now I was rattled by this set of incredible coincidences. *This is more like the Twilight Zone.* Startled, I handed her cash and walked out without waiting for change. My mind raced. *What is happening? Is this some kind of message in code?* I remembered I had demanded "a sign" from the floor of the prayer room. Were these signs? Was someone or something communicating with me?

Several weeks passed, and life went on as usual—except the 11:11's continued to appear, dozens of times a week. I had no greater understanding than when they first began. It got to the point where they were a normal part of my day. I pushed all questions to the back of my mind. No one knew much about my private life, so I had no one to tell about the "numbers" situation.

During that period, my stress continued to mount. The person I lived with needed immediate intervention. Their struggle with multiple addictions had begun creating havoc at their job and affecting other peoples' lives. Getting them admitted to a treatment center, when they were raging and resistant, was incredibly difficult. But eventually, with a friend's help, I was able to convince them to admit themselves for treatment.

As I left the rehab center, I became very emotional. I was exhausted from carrying so much for so long, and my life was filled with questions. On the way back to the hotel, as I approached a railroad crossing, the alarm began sounding. I stopped well before the crossing bar came down.

With a few moments to wait, I laid my forehead on the steering wheel and began weeping. The train rumbled by its vibrations shaking my rental car. Suddenly, the train horn blasted loudly, startling me. I lifted my head and looked up.

Across every passing boxcar was a large set of white numbers… 1111.

This cannot be real. I must be hallucinating from the stress, I thought. But the numbers were right there in front of me. There was no denying it. These numbers that had been plaguing my life for weeks and now they were rushing by in front of me. *Am I having a mystical experience? No one will ever believe this. Does anyone else experience this?*

There was no point in sharing my experience of repeating numbers until I better understood what was occurring. More importantly, I needed to get back to South Carolina and figure out the next steps for the rest of my life. *What was I going to do?*

The moment I asked the question, I felt an immediate sense of knowing. Words formed in my head: *It's time to move on.* The message surprised me, but I recognized that I had received guidance.

Back home, I attempted to continue with life as normally as possible, but I was deeply grieving. Despite the hardships I'd endured in that relationship, letting go was a new experience. I also had responsibilities, including a young son to care for. I didn't want him to see me collapse. Fortunately, he'd be away on a school trip the following week, which might give me the space and time I needed to figure things out. The next day, after I dropped my son off at school, I was alone to feel everything I had been holding back.

The home was too big and too quiet. It felt lonely instead of comforting. This space held too many painful memories. I crawled into bed and buried my head under the pillows. I slept for eighteen hours.

When I awoke, the emotion came pouring forth in a flood that was overwhelming. The pain felt excruciating, gripping deeply within my core. It would not let go of me—maybe I was the one who would not let go. I still felt so tired. I moved in and out of sleep states, often waking to myself whispering, "Help me, God. Help me."

My body was too worn out to continue. The grief had exhausted my spirit.

I slept through the next few days and into each night, opening my eyes from time to time. When I did, certain numbers were always present on the clock. The only numbers I seemed to awaken to were either 11:00, 11:11 or 1:11. During this impossible week, the numbers were relentless.

By the end of that week, I felt angry. The numbers were frustrating me now. I became reluctant to look at the clock, but then I would feel pulled. I had to see if the numbers were still there. Every single time, the clock would be flashing 11:00, 11:11 or 1:11.

Was this mental illness? I questioned my reality. However, a deeper part of me felt calm and comforted. It was as if I knew I was being watched over in a loving way. I continually wondered, *Are you talking to me? God? Universe? Angels?*

Night after night, I woke up to either 11:11 or 1:11. When I ventured out, 11, 111 or 1111 would appear on all manner of things: license plates, mailboxes, billboards, addresses. The signs were everywhere. And I still had no idea what they meant.

Several more weeks passed. The appearance of 1:11 and 11:11 remained consistent and constant. In time, I simply noticed them when they appeared and moved on with my day without giving them further thought. I slipped back into "doing" my life, while allowing these strange occurrences to become a commonplace experience.

After a while, I began saying "Thank you" with each appearance.

Nearly four weeks later, I reached my wits end. After having gone to bed early one night, I awoke after a few hours. The clock was flashing…11:11. This time, I yelled, "Either tell me what you want with these numbers or make them stop!"

At that moment, a series of images flashed through my mind. I saw magazine covers titled *11:11*, and a line that said "Devoted to the Journey of the Soul." I saw a radio banner emblazoned with *11:11 Talk Radio*. I experienced images, a flipping-page preview of the premiere issue. I saw graphics, interviews, and articles. I could even read some of the words. I saw who was interviewed within that issue.

Next, a set of sacred symbols appeared individually and then moved to form a single image—which matched the image on the magazine covers. When the flashes ceased, I immediately realized that I knew what the 11:11's signified and what each sacred geometric circle meant. Inside myself, in my own voice, I heard, *Do this now. You will heal. Others will heal.*

It was only at that moment that I truly grasped how 11, 1:11 and 11:11 had been a series of communications designed to bring me to the point where I could believe this calling. A cosmic language had been guiding and prompting me. It was the answer to my request. I realized I had been heard and now I was being watched over, protected, and supported.

The universe wanted me to embark on a path of growth and healing for myself, which would overflow onto others if I allowed it to. This is what 11:11 stood for. I somehow knew to listen to my heart and avoid any negative thoughts or inclinations.

Still, I wondered, *If the Universe can communicate through numbers, how many other ways has it been speaking to me?* Once again, my inner voice said: *In all ways, and always.*

I sat upright in bed and whispered, "Why are you asking *me*?" My background was not in publishing or writing!

But now something had awakened in me. I felt inspired and ready to act. A new adventure would allow room for my creativity and a chance to create beauty. My world had felt ugly and meaningless for a long time: 11:11 presented a path to greater meaning.

The independent, confident, and social person I had been before marrying had faded away. I needed to find that person again and to see myself as beautiful, empowered, and strong. It was important to discover who I was beyond the relationship I had been in, without needing support or approval from anyone else.

I leapt out of bed. Not caring that it was now past midnight, I raced downstairs to the office and began typing what I had seen in my head. I sent emails inquiring about interviews with people I never imagined would respond, much less agree.

Over the next month, I compiled content and put together everything I had seen in the vision. To my surprise, the prominent individuals I asked for interviews said yes! I completed the word document of the first full issue of *11:11 Magazine* in September of 2007.

Once I had the content, I realized that graphics and layout needed to be done. I had no idea how to create graphics, much less the next steps of getting a magazine formatted, printed, or distributed. I suddenly needed a graphic designer! How could I look for someone, and hope I chose the right person?

All the wind in my sail deflated and I became overwhelmed by the thought of putting the magazine out. I didn't know what I was doing! I knew nothing about publishing and personal growth. I was in the beginning stages of my own personal growth. Who was I to put this out into the world?

Doubt and insecurity crept in, and I allowed them to take over. I turned my chair away from the computer, discouraged.

A small, digital clock sat on the bookshelf in the corner. It was flashing 11:11. A sign. Somehow, I knew everything was going to be alright. I thought about my prayer room experience and remembered that speaking out loud had prompted this whole chain of events. Now I spoke again: "I did what you asked. I don't know any graphic designers. If you want this magazine out in the world, you will have to bring the graphic designer to me."

I felt happy and let it go as I snapped off the lights and went to bed.

That night, a severe storm hit. Lightning knocked out the power and blew a couple of fuses. In the morning, I realized my computer had crashed. It had been plugged directly into the wall instead of the surge protector. Everything I had done in the month prior was wiped out, gone in an instant.

So much time and work, and material was gone! My despair returned. But surely, this was not the end. I flipped open the phone book to find help and my eye landed on "Computer Guru." That's what I needed! I felt an odd sensation in my belly. I figured, *I am Indian, it makes sense to call a guru.* This thought made me chuckle, so I called and arranged for someone to come the next day.

After several hours working with my computer, the technician gave me the grim news: the machine was irreparable. However, he might be able to restore and retrieve some files.

One document was retrievable: just one. The document was titled "1111." I felt relieved.

While packing up, the computer tech asked what I did, and I shared my inspiration to create a life-enhancement magazine titled *11:11*. He said he was delighted that he had been able to help. His next words astounded me.

"You know… I have a dear friend who is going through a tough time. This sounds like something that might be good for her. She could use extra money right now and a boost of positivity. She is a fabulous graphic designer. Let me give you her number. She would also be a great guide through the publishing process."

My heart began to race. What I had specifically asked for had been provided. The graphic designer was brought directly to me. The universe had supplied my need. I was happily surprised.

That was the moment a broader awareness began to awaken in my body. It seemed so clear that the universe had been having a direct and intimate conversation with me. The cosmos was co-creating this experience. And now I knew I could converse with the universe in a tangible way.

I also realized that things are not always as they appear. The storm had caused my computer to crash, but this turned out to be a blessing. Everything was happening for my greater good. I only needed to begin looking at life differently.

Most importantly, I realized that *asking* brought the signs forward. My action had kept the dialogue going. This became the initial foundation for what has gone on to become a magical, mystical experience of conversations with the universe.

My dialogue continued to encompass numbers, but also the awareness of so much more. I began to see and share the infinite ways the world speaks to us.

Simran

THE PENNY

*perched on the edge of the cement front porch in stunned silence, clutching the penny, my tears falling onto my clenched hand. Had my father's luck become mine now?

I'm not certain how long I sat there staring at the 1888 Indian Head penny, but when the stony iciness of the cement seeped into my bones, I came back to my surroundings. I gazed out over the lawn of my childhood home and my eyes came to rest on my father's old garage. The weathered boards looked worn and weary now, so different from the beautiful structure it had been when first constructed, all those years ago.

My father was born in the summer of 1907, in a rural area of North Carolina known for its tobacco crops. In 1916, his father died suddenly, leaving behind the nine-year-old boy and grieving widow to bear the burden of working the farm. In those days, it was not unusual for a young child to be pulled from school to plow the fields. In that fateful year, my father left the third grade, never to return to school. His contribution to the farm was vital and his young hands could not be spared, even if it meant he lost an education.

From that point forward, Dad never knew a childhood day without backbreaking work, but that's what folks did back then; they sacrificed and did whatever they had to do just to put food on the table and clothes on their bodies. He was given the luxury of one pair of shoes a year, so he often worked the tobacco fields in his bare feet. It might seem a cruel and unfair life for a child, but I assure you, his kind and generous mother loved him well. His surviving parent instilled humility, love, and gentleness in him, characteristics my father held onto his entire life.

My earliest childhood memory is of my father tossing me high into the air and catching me while I laughed and begged for more. He was a wonderful man who worked long hours at a local sawmill during the winter months and raised tobacco during the summer, never failing to provide for his family. By class standards, we were poor—but I don't remember ever feeling poor as a child. I always had enough to eat and new clothes for school. My parents relied on labor and ingenuity to make ends meet. We had a vegetable garden, chickens, and fresh eggs, and of course, a milk cow.

My life in the country was fun, free, and rewarding, with summer days spent fishing at a neighbor's pond, picking wild blackberries and muscadine grapes by the bucketful, and riding my bicycle up and down the country roads. We caught fireflies after dark and enjoyed the best that country life could offer.

My parents bought my childhood home when I was three years old. They had never owned a home before; they had worked as sharecroppers in lieu of paying rent at their previous residence. I had no memory of that earlier house, but I often heard them talk about that time in their life. They told stories about working the fields of tobacco and wheat. My favorite stories were the ones about harvest time and meeting with all the surrounding neighbors at a central location to thresh and winnow the grain.

Threshing and winnowing took several days, so each family brought food, quilts, sawbucks, and lumber, the latter for building makeshift tables to hold the food: fried chicken, corn-on-the-cob, potato salad, cooked apples and a variety of breads and desserts. In the southern tradition, the women stood proudly by as the men and children got the first turn at the table.

Once the threshing and winnowing was complete, the bounty was hauled to a local gristmill for grinding into flour and the fresh, soft flour was evenly divided among all the families. Of course, a portion of the flour that my parents received went to their landlord as rental payment. On one occasion, the landlord asked my father if he would repair the kitchen floor in lieu of that month's rent; of course, my father eagerly accepted the offer. He spent days prying up the old floorboards. At times, he worked waist deep in the kitchen floor as he stood on the ground beneath the house to reinforce the joists. These were stories my parents often told. The tales implanted themselves in my memory because they illustrated the sacrifice and ingenuity it took to survive as poor, country folk.

My father passed away on a hot July day in 1991. Life as I knew it changed forever. The family's patriarch was gone and so was a piece of my heart. The world felt surreal. How could this sweet man be lost, and how would I survive losing him? My suffering paled in comparison to my mother's grief and hopelessness. She had spent fifty-five years with her beloved partner and didn't know how to go on without him.

I focused on Mom's well-being. She remained at my childhood home for eight additional years without the love of her life, but it soon became apparent that she needed a smaller place closer to the city and closer to me, because I had become her primary caregiver. In the spring of 2000, I found her a small apartment in a senior living facility about three miles from my house. Her new home did not have nearly enough space for all her furniture and personal belongings; we realized that an auction would be the best way to sell the remaining household items. For several weeks, I scrubbed the house, dragged the furniture around, and spruced up everything in preparation for the auction.

On the day before the auction, I drove out to the country to conduct a final walk-through, just to make certain everything was in order and ready for the next day. I lingered in the house, absorbing the familiar surroundings and saying one last good-bye to the home I had known for more than thirty years. Reluctantly, I opened the front door to leave. As I heard the click of the door latching into place, a voice called out to me—not my voice and not through my ears, but a man's voice inside my head! It said "Find that penny! Find that penny!" over and over. The speaker sounded insistent.

I moved like a zombie, stunned and not in control of my movements as I opened the door again. The voice in my head kept demanding, "Find that penny!"

I walked straight into my parents' bedroom and turned toward a bookshelf mounted on the wall near the big bed. As though controlled by an unseen force, I reached up to the top shelf where I touched a small, plastic container, which I tossed onto the bed.

The container was stuffed full of colorful spools of thread, needles, dusty old buttons, and a thimble. I dug down to the bottom and saw a coin lying there—and at that very moment, the voice stopped. I snatched up the coin, shoved the container back into its place, and left the house again, locking the door behind me.

As I sat on the edge of the porch, turning the coin—which was nearly worn smooth—over with trembling fingers, I knew at the deepest level of my soul that my discovery had great significance. That's what brought me to tears. I could still recall the voice that had directed me. Now I realized it had been my father's voice! For whatever reason, he had led me to find this penny.

I gathered myself and hurried home so I could call my mother to tell her what had happened. I was still emotional from the event and my mother could tell that something important had happened as I said hello. I could barely stammer through the details, but as soon as I finished, she said, "You found daddy's penny?" Her voice was in disbelief.

She went on to tell me a story I hadn't heard before.

My father had found the penny when he replaced that kitchen floor in the house they'd rented, decades earlier. As he stood waist deep, working on the floor joists, something shiny caught his eye on the ground below. He thought it might be a lost button that had fallen through the cracks of the floor, but when he bent down and retrieved the object, he saw that it was an 1888 Indian Head penny.

"He considered that coin a good luck piece and carried it in his pocket for decades," Mom said.

The penny looked newer then, she added, but became worn because Dad often rubbed it between his fingers. "He never went anywhere without it."

"Why didn't I know about this penny for all those years?"

"Your father was afraid one of you kids might lose it if you knew about it."

But then it was lost anyway. "One day, shortly before he died," Mom said, "he told me he had misplaced the penny. We searched for hours, but finally gave it up for lost."

Now my mother began to cry, saying, "I can't believe you found that penny! Daddy would be so happy!"

When I told her I felt it was daddy's voice that led me to the penny, she agreed.

Finding that lucky penny had relied on Divine timing. Had I not gone out to the house the evening before the auction, the talisman would have been lost forever. My father had reached out to me from the other side and led me to find something he considered a small treasure.

I still have his good luck charm today. It is more precious to me than anything else in the world—because it was a gift from my beloved father.

Pamela D. Nance

BLINKING LIGHTS AND DRAGONFLIES

*I*t wasn't the first time I'd gotten a sign from my beloved late husband. He had been the love of my life and my best friend, but he'd lost a long battle with cancer. After his transition, I couldn't bear to live in my house another minute without him, and my daughters and I began staying at my sister's house, a few blocks away. Relocating gave us a temporary break from the constant stream of compassionate visitors.

I returned one night to grab a few of our things. Alone in the house in the quiet evening, I broke down. My skin became icy, and chills ran through my body. I rested my head on the windowsill and sobbed, "Will I ever be okay?"

Just then, I noticed the floodlight in the yard blink off and then on again! Puzzled, I whispered again, "Will we be okay?"

It happened again. I thought, *This can't be possible!* But after the third time, I knew the light was a sign. It was my husband saying, *Yes! Be bright. Let our light shine. Be the light!*

I smiled as I felt all the love we had shared. Suddenly, I knew the girls and I would return to our home and begin our new lives.

We decided to focus on travel instead of sadness that summer, traveling to New York City, California, and Alaska to visit family and friends. I wanted the girls to see the big world we live in, rather than focusing on grief. Then it was time to start the new school year. As we got out of the car after the first day of school, several dragonflies encircled us. We laughed and wondered ... *Could they be a sign, too?*

A few of the gem-colored beauties became a swarm, and as we entered the house, they all flew in with us. The girls thundered around the house giggling and opening all the doors to encourage our insect guests to fly back out.

They started screaming, "Be free, little dragonflies!" After a bit of play, the dragonflies flew back outside.

We'd been through so many changes over the summer, and we welcomed the small things that made us laugh and play.

After that, my daughters would say "Hi, Daddy!" whenever they saw dragonflies. They believed it was their sign that their father was with them at that moment.

Then came a day, later that month, when the whole country was hit with tragedy. I was at the elementary school of which I was a founder and where my daughters attended school. As I stood on the playground with the preschool class, the area suddenly filled with dragonflies. The children ran around calling them and playing with such happy hearts—but I saw the other teacher approaching me with tears filling her eyes, visibly shaken. She leaned toward my ear and whispered to get the children inside, as we were entering a countywide lockdown. A plane had just crashed into the towers in NYC, and another was headed for Washington, DC. Our country was under attack, and it was our job to protect the children in our small community.

All I could think of was, *But the dragonflies were here ... for laughter and fun ...*

We hurried inside as we waited for the devastating news of September 11, 2001 to unfold. We decided to send everyone home. In our car, my oldest daughter said she was grateful that we had seen the towers before they went down.

"Mommy," she said, "a lot of children lost their parents today. We aren't the only ones without a Daddy."

Her words broke my heart, but they also made me realize that the dragonflies had visited that day to remind the children of hope. They symbolized the souls who had not forgotten them. They wanted to encourage them to laugh and play.

Flashing lights have turned up as signs for our family through the years. Each new home we have lived in over the past twenty years has had moments where lights inexplicably shut off and blink back on again. We always reply, "We miss you, we love you, Daddy. Thank you, Daddy!"

The dragonflies still follow us and land on our toes and our fingers at the most interesting times. It happened once when my youngest daughter was in a fiercely competitive college softball game. The score was close. My daughter was up to bat.

Suddenly, a dragonfly alighted briefly, gently on the tip of her bat. She called time out and broke into laughter as the umpire asked in astonishment, "Did you see that?"

Then she smacked the ball with a powerhouse hit that changed the trajectory of the game.

Yes, we had seen it, and my family all knew the power of that sign. We will always recognize that reminder of laughter and play!

Jennifer Perez Solar

NEVER ALONE

The snow was falling as fast as the temperature. The treacherous conditions kept most people off the roads that night, but as a teenager, I didn't know enough to be afraid.

At sixteen years old, the devastation of my dad's recent, unexpected death—followed shortly by abuse from a trusted friend—had spiraled me into a reckless and dangerous place. No blizzard was going to hold me back! I was headed for a party where I could numb my suffocating pain.

And then, with only a few miles to go, I rounded a corner and my car started spinning, out of control, just like my life. It felt like the spinning was never going to end…just like my pain.

Once the car stopped, I was afraid to open my eyes. When I did, I couldn't see much ahead of me through the white-out conditions. But somehow, up above, I saw the neon canopy lights of a gas station. To my left, a gas pump sat right outside my window, as if I had pulled up to fill my tank. My head dropped to the steering wheel, and I started sobbing—partly out of fear and partly out of relief. I started begging God for a reason my world was collapsing around me.

I felt the largest, warmest, most comfortable blanket in the world being wrapped around my shivering body and heard a whisper assuring me I was going to be okay. My emotions switched from despair to something I had lost over the previous few months—hope. I felt an enormous, protective, and loving presence in my car that night, a beautiful sign assuring me that I was not alone.

Thirty years passed. The numbers 111, 1111, and 333 started appearing at least a dozen times a day, but I had no idea of their meaning—until I awoke at 3:33 one morning with piercing pains in my left breast. My doctor did not feel any lumps, and he was optimistic that the pain was a side effect of too little sleep and too much caffeine.

I was diagnosed with breast cancer a few weeks later. It took a year of surgery and other aggressive treatments to become cancer free. I sometimes asked the universe to send me white feathers to confirm everything would be okay—and they showed up in crazy, unexpected places like bathrooms, my office, and in my car. One time, a white feather even gently floated down from the sky, landing directly on my arm.

As many people do when they feel their mortality, I began to think a lot about my life's purpose. I had a perfect life: a successful career and an incredible family and circle of friends. Yet I felt a huge hole in my life that nothing could seem to fill. Then, during a business trip to New York City in December 2019, I somehow received the mystical sign I needed.

It was the holiday season, and I snapped photos of sparkling lights and magnificent decorations. In one photo, the time on a digital clock in the background read "13:89." *That is not a time*, I thought. Since it was a "live" photo that captured a few seconds of video, I saw the display changing to thirty-six degrees after a couple seconds and then back to the correct time of 11:04. The number 13:89 never showed up on another picture. I knew this number was intended as a direct message for me.

According to my research, the numerical sequence 1389 means "one door is beginning to open as another is closing." The sign was urging me to listen to my intuition, which was leading me to my true soul's calling. Chills ran throughout my body. I was mentally and emotionally exhausted from my career and ready to leave. *Was this the closing door?*

I found a less stressful job. While walking in for my final interview, a beautiful rainbow appeared over the building signaling that I was in the right place. I began to relax—until the night my bedside lamp started flickering, as if to get my attention.

I blurted out, "Seriously, if you are trying to communicate with me, stop flashing and let me know."

Just as the flickering stopped, I heard another voice saying, *Enough is enough.*

Utterly confused, I begged for more signs, but nothing emerged. Months later, I finally understood. *I* was enough! It was time to focus on me, so that everyone would get a better version of me, and I could serve them better. Serving others brings me joy—it's my true life's purpose. The answer was always there. I just needed to stop asking outside sources for it and become fully present within myself long enough to hear it.

The universe wanted me to stop procrastinating and write the book I'd been talking about for twenty years.

Shortly after that revelation, an email showed up asking for story submissions on how signs have influenced my life. I knew it was the first step, which is always the most critical step in any journey.

When I see a sign now, I simply smile and receive it with gratitude. Those Divine guideposts that have helped me navigate through my toughest times and even steered me in the direction of my true calling. I no longer need blaring alarms or flashing lights, just a little time to listen to my inner voice—the voice that will always guide me where my soul is destined to go. It's comforting to know I am never alone.

V.L. Cessna

PROPHETIC OPPORTUNITIES

*A*s I picked wild dandelions, I saw a sudden flash of brilliant light in front of me. The yellow dandelions disappeared and were replaced by rows and rows of white dandelions. I didn't find this particularly scary or exciting. I was six years old and already accustomed to using my imagination to break up the monotony of life in my small town. I envisioned places of wonder, places of play, and places where no one could bother me. The rest of my life was all chores and homework.

As I watched the white dandelions in my mind's eye, like a motion picture, I saw my cousin Chris riding his motorcycle and then being hit by a car! Chris slid to the side of the road; he seemed to survive, but his motorcycle was destroyed.

Naturally, this violent vision shocked me. Why would my imagination have created such a sight? Oddly enough, I wasn't frightened. I raised my eyebrows and thought, *Wow–that was interesting!* and proceeded to make my way home.

I told my mother about my experience in the field. She was not impressed and didn't accept it as well as I did. She cuffed me on the head and said, "You are *never* to repeat that story! It was the devil's work."

I was so young! How could she have said I was evil? I knew she believed in the devil, and now she was telling me that I had the devil in me. I felt sad about this development, but I didn't tell anyone else about my vision. I obeyed my mother like a "good girl" does.

Two weeks later, as I sat at the dining table, my father announced that my cousin Chris had been in a motorcycle accident. He had survived, but the bike was destroyed.

My vision hadn't been the devil's work at all. It had been the truth! I felt joyful that I'd had the opportunity to peer into the future, even if I needed to keep it to myself.

My guides have been with me through the years that followed, and because of the frequency of their visits, I became quite astute at dealing with the prophecies. My visions became second nature to me. But they could not prepare me for the startling vision to come.

My husband and I were on vacation, along with our two children—then aged eight and six—in New York City. We had gone to a pizza joint for dinner and headed back to the apartment to bathe the children and get them into bed. We watched yet another Disney movie for good measure. I recall feeling particularly happy and content—my life was so good. I fell asleep easily, my heart full of gratitude.

At precisely four a.m., someone nudged me awake. I assumed it was my husband or one of the kids—but I opened my eyes to see the most beautiful, luminous angel I had ever witnessed, next to me. She was transparent yet possessed incredibly blue piercing eyes. Was she a ghost?

She motioned for me to sit up in bed, and I did. She wanted to converse with me and immediately announced that she meant no harm. *I come in joy and peace*, she said. *I was summoned by your vibrational offering and your abundant and joyful feeling before you fell asleep.*

I felt complete awe, but no fear. I glanced over at my husband, sound asleep and totally oblivious to my visitor.

I listened carefully, although her brightness and beauty mesmerized me. She was articulate, and every word held meaning. She wasn't wasting any time.

My name is Sophie, and I am your primary Spirit Guide. I have been with you since your first premonition at age six. I have worked with you since that time, and it is a pleasure to come to you now. I am representing seven other energies of the Light, and I come with a proposed mission for you. We need you to spread the word of our existence, because the world is in desperate need of help. We need you to utilize your skills (and we will help you hone those skills even further) to help and serve people on planet Earth.

She then showed me a vision of a white van. She said I would be buying this van, which would be a gift from her and the other energies she represented. She indicated that I was to drive this van everywhere I could, to talk about spirit guides and how they are benevolent and helpful.

I was initially confused, but I felt oddly at peace with these messages. When Sophie asked if I would accept the mission, I wholeheartedly affirmed that I would.

It was a surreal experience. It was an exhilarating experience. I suspect it lasted only a few minutes. As Sophie was preparing to leave, my son—then age six—awoke and propped himself up in his bed, which was on the other side of the same room.

"Mama, do you see what I see?" he whispered.

"Yes," I replied.

"Is she here to talk to you or to talk to me?"

"Me."

"Okay," he said, and promptly went back to sleep.

I didn't tell my husband about this experience at first. I wanted to treasure the beauty and magnificence of my initial introduction to Sophie for a while. Yet oddly enough, when we got back from New York, my husband purchased a new vehicle—a white family van.

Deep down, I began to realize that each premonition, including those I now received from Sophie, were signs for me to follow my path. Even the white van was a sign of confirmation, reminding me to keep trusting in my gifts and voice. I would be guided each step of the way.

My son proved to be another sign. He had seen my guide! I knew now that others could have the experience I had. Many people are born with gifts, but some are taught to trust them, and others to fear them.

I recalled my mother's response to my first premonition, and I decided my response to my son would be entirely different. This definitely wasn't the devil's work.

Elizabeth Parojcic

FLOATING FREELY

hroughout the years as I went through relationships and career shifts, feathers and birds were consistent signs for me. Spirit was showing up in my life and I learned that I was being guided, even when I felt directionless.

As I drove, birds would swoop in front of my car. While hiking, I would sit on a mountain top and watch a single bird, soaring calmly through the mountain tops, and feel there was a message there. Sometimes birds would fly into my home, perch on a windowsill, and then whisk themselves out the door again. After it happened several times, I knew it was Spirit speaking to me.

What could the birds be trying to tell me? I began to watch their behavior and open my heart to their messages. Sometimes the message was, *It's time to be free, it's time to soar, it's time to have fun, it's time to simply float freely.* I began to discover feathers in the most random, unexpected places. Sometimes I'd see a feather dropping from the sky, but I also noticed them in the decorations in other peoples' homes and in businesses.

As I walked into new phases of life, feathers appeared in my path to give me comfort, validation, and encouragement. A feather meant that I was headed in the right direction, that I wasn't alone, and that Spirit was guiding me on my unknown, evolving path.

In December of 2010, something had awakened within me and prompted a major decision. Pieces of me had withered away as I became a multitasking machine. My actions, my words, and my life became robotic. I realized that I was now willing to do whatever it took to heal. I wanted to really live, perhaps for the first time. I'd been drifting through life on autopilot—and that had to end.

Now I had a mission: to learn about my patterns, beliefs, and behaviors. I wanted to discover myself on levels I'd never dreamed possible. I was committed to heal.

I began 2011 knowing it would be a year of monumental growth and change. This was the year I started to feel connected to life again.

I quickly learned that not everyone would understand me or my journey, or the new decisions I was being led to make. Now when the feathers showed up, I would hear messages, from Spirit saying, *It's time to discover your sense of self. Dare to be you! When you have the courage to speak up, be vulnerable.*

I now give others permission to do the same. Authenticity is liberating.

My encounters with signs led me to deeper insights about myself, my roles, and my strengths. I examined my life by asking the important questions: "Where have I found real purpose in living? What are my talents and natural abilities? Where am I most effective, efficient, and productive?"

The answers pointed me in the direction I needed to go.

The older I have become, the easier it is to see that my life has been a combination of suffering and joy. Of course, we all want the happy times— but I now realized that my seasons of despair had brought me closer to God. All my experiences had led me to living more by *being* and less by *doing*.

I had to rethink my definition of success and ponder some key questions:

"What if I never built an empire or dominated an industry, or rose to the top of anything? What if I built a simple life that was generative and supportive? What if I felt satisfied in the right here, right now?"

Changing the filter through which I viewed my life made everything more vibrant. I found that my life was closer to ideal than I had ever thought.

Just last week, I was meditating near a lake in Colorado Springs, and I heard Spirit ask *How much more space would your joy have if you stopped thinking you had to earn it?*

I felt encouraged to embrace my life and to simply be me.

And then I saw feathers floating in the sky.

Brigitte Bartley Sawyer

NEW YEAR'S NIGHT

*E*ach New Year, revelers would arrive in the little fishing village called Alligator Pond on the south coast of Jamaica, where I lived. Alligator Pond was always a colorful place, with its extensive fishing boats of red, yellow, and green. Mama's bright yellow house on the sand hill had a big mango tree in the front yard and overlooked the ocean. From the front window, I watched the fishing boats on the sea and Mama and the other women sitting on the beach, waiting for their fishermen to return.

To celebrate New Year's Day, people from all over the island came to Alligator Pond. They rode in on motorcycles, drove vans, or hired private buses to get to the party. Some even walked from nearby communities. Our town square was lit with green and yellow lights, with an illuminated Ferris wheel churning in the middle as music blared from giant speakers. People strolled around from shop to shop or played board games. The visitors liked eating jerk chicken, curry goat with white rice, fried fish, bammy, bag juice, and roasted or boiled corn.

One year, when I was nine, I put on my new fancy yellow and red floral dress with my favorite red sandals and joined the children from Top Bay, another community in Alligator Pond, heading to the town square.

It was a sweltering night. I was excited until I saw the first carnival mask. Some visitors disguised themselves in those carnival masks to welcome the new year. Their faces were grotesque as they jumped around dancing, playing board games, and eating fried fish with bammy. I'd never seen a carnival mask in my small fishing village, and now they were everywhere! The masks seemed to be their real faces! Could they be supernatural beings who lived on Earth?

I felt cornered, trapped, and overwhelmed by fear. The other children were enjoying the party. Mama was talking with the other women from Top Bay. Nobody was paying any attention to me.

I made a quick decision to get away from all these people. I wanted to go home. I knew I could return to Top Bay by walking along the beach, although the road would have been faster. The beach was open and empty, and the waves were quiet at night, so I could walk without getting my dress wet. I decided to head toward Tee Zam, which was closer. I did not know that route very well, but I remembered Mama telling me I could reach it by walking on Tee Zam Road, past the Big Rock.

"When you get to Standpipe," she had said, "walk up the sand hill and you'll reach Top Bay."

This was all I knew. I did not think of anything else as I hurried down the beach.

I had left the town square without telling Mama or my friends from Top Bay, because she was still talking to the fabric vendor and my friends were enjoying their fried fish, cotton candy, and the popcorn with a purple ring inside the bag. I had dashed through the alleyway between the small shops, but I did not cry. I was courageous. Fear of all these strange people had frozen my tears in my eyes.

Mama always told me an angel would protect me wherever I went. No matter the situation I might find myself in, the angel would give me the courage and strength to deal with it. I also knew that the Father in Heaven could see me walking alone in the darkness, heading for Top Bay.

Had I had left my angel behind at the celebration? I felt great sorrow for not having brought him with me. But I knew that my angel saw and knew everything. Surely, he would notice me walking alone on Tee Zam Road.

As I was about to reach Big Rock, a large, tall woman wearing a carnival mask appeared. I can still see her flashing eyes in my imagination. She approached me from the side of the rock and grabbed my hand. At that moment, I could have died from fright! I didn't know what was happening. Where had this woman come from? She clutched my hand so tightly that it began to ache as she pulled me back to the town square.

I had walked a few steps, held prisoner in this woman's hand, when I felt a powerful sensation through my body. Someone else had arrived. I knew him to be present as truly as I knew the presence of the big, masked woman on my other side. It was my angel, the one Mama always talked about. My Father in Heaven had sent this angel to protect me and take me home.

I couldn't see him, but I was aware of his presence walking beside me. I felt that if I could see him, he'd be wearing bright colors of yellow and green. The absolute certainty that he was at my side made me feel calm. I felt like I was surrounded by pure, white light, as if I were standing directly under a large spotlight on a stage.

The masked woman freed me with a push, and I did not see her again. She disappeared into the crowd. I walked back through the alleys, between the makeshift shacks that the visitors built. I mentally thanked my angel, and we enjoyed a short but pleasant conversation as I searched for Mama. It was like a conversation between two close friends. My angel walked with me through the crowds, and the carnival masks no longer frightened me.

I couldn't wait to tell Mama about the encounter I had with my angel. All the fear exited my body, and my soul was filled with sweet tranquility.

The next morning when I woke up, I felt totally at peace with myself and everyone else in the world, and free of stress, anxiety, and fear.

A few days later, I was walking on the beach heading for school when I started thinking about my "new friend" and how protected I had felt. When I reached Big Rock, I sensed his presence again. I told him that I was grateful that he had reappeared, and we walked together on the beach.

After that, I had no more fear of walking on Tee Zam road and passing Big Rock. I called my protector my "new friend" until the age of fourteen, when I learned that he was my guardian angel.

I always understood him perfectly when he spoke to me, although I never heard his voice. He was the loving presence that led me home.

Patricia Ewers

A PROMISE UNDER THE WISTERIA

I t was a Christmas night without church, without carols, without mistletoe. The world was drowned in darkness around me, but there was still a faint glimmer of hope in the placid sky. It whispered that perhaps the feather was light and soft, the doves could spread their wings, and the rare songbirds were not losing their love melodies.

I had reserved a spot in the Koyasan Okunoin Night Tour and found myself strolling among the dead in a cemetery of 200,000 believers of the monks of Kukai. Only five people were in our intimate group; the foreign tourists were lost in the mystery of the shadows of the night.

Deep in a dusky forest, a long, enchanting path was lit up by a snow-covered row of stone lanterns. Their yellow-orange glow lit the pilgrims' path. The resting place of Kukai was alive with his legend, his teaching, and his spirit.

"Namu-Daishi-Henjō-Kongō," I chanted with an unwavering heart and sweet conviction. A crow broke the silence, as if carrying my prayer beyond the threshold of the sacred.

Lonely Christmas.

Okunoin.

Kukai.

They all made sense now.

And this was only a prelude to the true calling of my journey. The next day, after a hearty breakfast at the Kokuu Guesthouse, my journey to the west began. I found myself strolling in Okunoin again. Snow must have paid an unannounced visit during the mountain's sleep the previous night. The all-white cemetery, softly lit by the golden inks of the morning sun, was veiled with a profound, mysterious sense of unspoken beauty.

Strolling along the less-trodden paths was a purification rite. With unadulterated joy, I continued my way to Shojoshinin, Karukayado, Kongobuji Temple, Danjo Garan Complex and Sainanin. Midway in the journey, I stopped by Daishi Kyokai and received Jukai. The ceremony was performed in a completely dark hall, and all devoted attendees treaded to the center of the stage, softly and laggardly. I sat on the tatami floor and made my best effort to recite after the monk. It was my second time receiving Jukai. It still felt sacred, but less powerful than my first Jukai, back in the time when Koyasan was celebrating its 1,200-year anniversary.

I knelt in front of the altar and listened attentively. Tears kept rolling down my cheeks, though I barely understood the monk's teaching. Profound purification, I surmised.

The journey continued. Daimon, a huge, multi-storied gate in the west, was the destination on my itinerary. The sky was getting dark, and the scent of the air told me the rain would start soon. I just had one goal: to reach the gate before I got caught in a downpour.

But life is full of distractions. My eyes were drawn to a *torii* leading to a park. Across the road, the park looked small and humble—it wouldn't take me more than five minutes to glance around. I crossed the road before I found a bridge over a tiny pond upon passing the *torii*. The unpeopled park was spacious with a wisteria in the middle. Wisteria in winter is neither showy nor bodacious.

I was about to turn and leave when a staircase to my far right appeared out of nowhere. It was no phantasm of the imagination. Feeling destined, I walked up without giving it much thought. The air was pristine and sweet. Ahead of me, the long flight of steps ascending to the Haraikawa Benten Shrine was festooned with lily-of-the-valley. These drooping clusters of delights, as if out of winter's reach, greeted me happily. The ambience up there was very alive—so alive that an image of its antithesis popped into my mind.

In a flash, I saw the stream that once flowed swiftly next to Mihashira Torii in a Kyoto shrine shrouded in silence. The place had lost the voices of the well; the maiden had gone and the Earth was barren. But in here, the paradigm of an immemorial harmony flowered into being, and the air carried a melody that was harmonious and euphonious. My heart sang. Next to the Benten Shrine were two shrines dedicated to Inari Daimyojin. I paid my respect to the deities, feeling blessed for this bond, while contemplating upon the founding story of Mount Koyasan and the merging of Esoteric Buddhism and Shintoism.

As I went down the stairs, I saw some lovely little stones along the way. My teacher had suggested I collect twelve stones during my trip, for the later shamanic ceremonies. Timidly, I asked the deities if I could gather stones from this place and take them back to Hong Kong. I received a yes, but a vague one.

I picked up the shining stones with a nod and gently put them in a white pouch. A chasm of doubt and uncertainty stretched between the stones and me. What if I had interpreted the message incorrectly? What if the stones preferred to stay on this mountain?

I decided to ask once more. I put the pouch on a table sheltered by the wisteria and placed on top of it a small tree branch.

"Dear deities of Koyasan, may I have your permission to carry the stones back to my home city? If yes, could you move the branch away from its original position? If no, could you make the branch stay still? I will be back for your oracle after visiting Daimon. Thank you."

Half an hour later, I made my way back. Just as I stood under the wisteria, the heavens opened. The branch had moved from its original position. Whether it was the deities, the wind, or other people—the sign was clear. I gave thanks and continued my journey before the rain fell.

Mount Koyasan is a landscape steeped in stories. Old stories have been reclaimed, and new stories will weave our dreaming. The stones sit quietly and patiently on my altar, ready for the next ceremony.

Joanna Lai

EDNA AND THE BIRCH

*a*s I step onto the trail, the frigid January wind stings my cheeks and bites my legs through my jeans, but I know I need to walk. It's all I've been able to do since my father died, just before Christmas. Today is no different, so I force my legs forward into the woods, grateful there is no snow covering the trail.

Immediately, the energy around me shifts, as if the space is electrically charged. Holly trees thickly line the path with their deep green leaves and brilliant red berries; they offer a kind of peace and protection that eases the tension I have been carrying, allowing me to soften just a little. Tall pine trees sway and bend above me in the wind. Stopping to listen to their branches move, I pray they might have a message for me, something to comfort me.

Be gentle and kind with yourself, I hear—or at least, I think I do.

Deeper into the woods, I find myself drawn to a huge oak. In its bark, I can see the outline of a face, like one of those decorations people might attach to a tree. I reach toward its smiling face and gently place my gloved hands onto its bark. Then I slowly stretch my arms around it as if it were a long-lost friend. I have never been a tree-hugger before, but here I am, tightly holding onto this oak. Its power pushes against me, but not in a harsh way. I'm not sure if I feel fear or awe, but I lean in again. The world around me fades from awareness. All that's left is this powerful, grounded tree and me. Its gentle strength pours a kind, caring, gentle love into every cell of my being.

I feel like a broken-hearted child, and the tree is an ancient, wise, loving father or grandfather who has reached down to pick me up and hold me on his knee. I am safe. My tears flow without judgment, without shame, without question. I am not alone in my grief now. There is such profound wisdom, yet such simplicity, in this message. I let go of the tree but keep a hand against its trunk and pick up a small acorn lying at my feet.

"Thank you," I whisper, tucking the acorn into my pocket so I won't forget, yet in the deepest parts of my knowing, I understand that this encounter was real.

As I walk back to the car, I recall the maple tree that grew in front of my grandparents' summer cottage. My grandmother was very protective of that tree. She frequently scolded my cousins and me for clambering up its trunk onto its sturdy branches.

"Don't you kids damage that bark!" she'd holler. She could often be found sitting beside the maple, sipping coffee from an old ceramic mug, a lit cigarette dangling from her fingers, gazing at its beauty. She seemed happiest when she was connected to that tree in a way I didn't comprehend back then.

I spent so much of my childhood leaping off our porch railing and crash landing into piles of fall leaves. I loved the sweet, musky smell of the leaves when they were first released from their branches, before they became dry and brittle. That scent still transports me somewhere far away.

Now, with the arrival of spring, I find myself needing to commune with the trees again. It's an eerily familiar feeling that I can't quite explain, so I test the sanity of it with a friend who is deeply connected to the healing found in nature.

"I feel a calling to be with the trees," I tell her. "It's like a deep longing to be with them. I feel like I need to take a pilgrimage of sorts."

"Of course, you do," she says with a mischievous smile that suggests she knows something I do not, as if she had just been waiting for me to feel this kind of connection. Somehow, she knows I need the "medicine" of being with the trees.

Heeding the call, I arrive at the parking area of the Atlantic White Cedar Swamp Trail. My heart sinks at the sight of four other cars in the parking lot. A Wednesday morning in April used to mean the promise of quiet walks alone, without the tourists Cape Cod expects in summer, but I remember now how much times have changed here.

I can hear only bird songs and the rustling of creatures on the ground, scurrying here and there with the business of their day, as I start toward the wooded area. Minding each step on the uneven, pine-needle path, I arrive at the head of the trail and step onto the boardwalk, entering their world.

Cedars and maples stretch up out of swampy water on both sides of the wooden boardwalk. Sunlight flickers through their branches, and their beauty is reflected in the water, which looks clear and elegant rather than murky. I exhale the breath I didn't realize I had been holding and sink down onto a nearby bench. My tears begin to fall.

Summoning courage, I ask the trees what I came to ask. "Can you tell me about letting go? About grief?"

It's about release. You must loosen, not tighten, a deep, strong, gentle voice answers, and I am startled by the immediacy of their response.

"I think I understand," I whisper.

I realize that I have spent my entire life tightening around loss. So many tragedies are hidden instead of being released, because of the world's discomfort with pain. I have always tried to hold tightly, clinging to what I had lost. It's been difficult learning to find enough safety and comfort to release my pain.

It is in the releasing that space opens for the very love you have been trying to hold onto. Loosening is what allows for the holding of what's precious. The very thing that you're craving. That is the paradox: To hold on, we must release. Simple. Not easy.

I thank these tree spirits and somehow understand that they have said all they will for now. The creaking from a tree bending with the wind draws my attention. Leaning against it is a smaller, dead tree. It holds the dead tree against it as a mother would her child. It has let go, released, so it can now hold on with love.

Passing another tree with a huge, bulbous growth halfway up its trunk, as if it imploded as it grew, I hear the word, *Disease.*

"But you kept growing beyond that," I say.

Exactly.

Another tree whispers that I should not fear any of this and that it is safe to keep going.

Just then, a family comes up from behind and passes me, discussing their plans for the rest of the day. Right behind them is a couple walking their dog. They stop, and while I pet the curly brown Goldendoodle, we chat about dogs and hiking for a moment. I hang back as they move on, wanting the space to myself again.

Suddenly, the woman with the dog appears before me again. "Isn't this place magical? It really is special. I just love it!" she says, as though she could sense my own reaction to these woods. She understands the connection and magic I am feeling here. And just as quickly as she appeared, she is gone, catching up with her family again.

The wind is picking up, and trees continue creaking as they bend and sway. A very tall cedar, to my left and deeper into the woods, creaks loudly above the others with an almost ancient moaning. She tells me her name is Edna and explains that she moaned so I would notice her. My heart fills with love and a deep recognition. I remember the kind of love I felt from the oak tree, months ago.

"Why did you want me to notice you?" I ask.

Look closer, she encourages.

I see a birch tree in front of her bending forward and back again, slightly touching her as it does. I smile at the sweetness they seem to share. I love birch trees. My friend tells me I remind her of a birch, which is one of the first species to regrow in places of tragedy. Birches can thrive in harsh conditions and colder climates. It's also one of the first trees to regrow leaves after the winter, bringing the new life of spring.

You see, Edna continues, *like this birch before me, I have stood with you throughout time. Now, you are here and can see and feel it.*

I do feel it—a loving strength and support. Her wisdom is so clear, and I feel confident enough to ask for her advice about the work I want to do with people and their grief, the retreats I want to offer.

She answers immediately, *You can do this anywhere. There is no need to get stuck in the where questions you ask. Wherever people are, you can do the work. Just bring it to them.*

"How?" I ask, still grasping for answers.

She lets out a long, slow, creaking moan, like an old woman whose bones ache from arthritis as she rises from her chair. *Just as you are. Relax. Patience. All in due time, child.*

I feel her wisdom profoundly and her gentle, loving way. "Thank you, Edna," I offer with profound respect.

She says nothing more, but I can feel her love and caring support within me.

I move forward a few steps but hesitate, not wanting to leave. Finally, taking another step, I notice a cedar next to Edna. The two of them stand together like two old friends or lovers who have lived a long life together. They sway in unison, supporting the birch in front of them, knowing each other in a way that requires no words. I'm touched by what they share. They've experienced a lifetime of growing, each on their own, yet together, side by side. Genuine love.

Go slow and be gentle with yourself, Edna calls with one last creak.

"Can you come with me somehow, so I can talk to you even when I can't come here?" I ask, not wanting to leave her.

She laughs. *Remember child, I am always with you, always have been. I have watched over you forever and will watch over you always. I am happy you have opened enough to allow me to connect with you like this. Now we will be together wherever you go.*

Exhaling gratitude, I walk slowly away from Edna and the birch, thanking them and all the cedars for their guidance, trusting all that we shared. I am at peace, gently comforted and supported. The edges of my own pain have been softened by their love.

As I drive home, I know this day with the trees has been everything I needed, exactly when I needed it. Forever touched by their grace and wisdom, I am blessed to know the spirit of the trees.

Mary-Elizabeth Briscoe

WHEN GOD SHOWED UP ON RODEO BEACH

"I want to die. I want to die. I want to die. I want to die."

This had become my mantra during the summer of 2017.

I was facing my second cancer diagnosis. I had successfully healed uterine cancer six years earlier without chemotherapy, surgery, or radiation by following my Divine guidance and taking an all-natural approach. In four short months, the cancer had vanished!

Elated by the experience of allowing God to guide me through a natural healing process, I lived cancer-free—until now. This recurrence bombarded my brain with relentless questions. *Why had it come back? Had it ever really gone away? Had it spread throughout my body?*

What had I done wrong?

The escalating, unanswered questions threw me into full fear mode as I thought, *I might have caused myself harm by healing naturally.*

For the medical concerns, I underwent CT scans, bone scans, genetic testing, and painful biopsies. For my mental anguish, I took myself to therapy. I visited energy healers, hypnotherapists, and spiritual teachers. One conclusion became increasingly apparent: Although there was cancer in my body, the real healing required wasn't physical.

After the first cancer had healed so quickly, I had celebrated and vowed to get to the root cause, so it would never come back again. That search uncovered painful, suppressed memories. And then the depression, which had been my close companion since age eleven, returned. Now the depression was strangling me and threatening my life.

In moments of clarity, I knew, deep down, that the cancer and depression had the same origin. The cancer had turned up in my uterus to show me where to look.

"Down here! Bring your focus down here," my body had whispered.

It takes a certain kind of wounded monster to sexually abuse a child. When I was a young girl, my brain couldn't comprehend it: How could a big human do something so harmful to a little human? I told myself that the man who hurt me was "not in his right mind."

But sadly, because of this unimaginable abuse, my mind wasn't right, either.

Yes, it takes a certain kind of wounded monster to hurt a child. But I now know it takes a certain kind of wounded warrior to overcome any kind of abuse. Through no choice of my own, I was tasked with becoming such a warrior.

The truth is, I didn't think I had it in me to face my deepest, most shameful pain while dealing with cancer. Not again. It felt too difficult to heal myself physically while also unraveling the decades-long battle in my mind. I realized I had made *my mind* the enemy, instead of identifying the monster as the enemy. What else would a helpless child know to do?

Now, the therapies I pursued revealed that I had no other choice: I would have to face the darkest recesses of my mind.

I drove myself to Rodeo Beach—my favorite spot—on a beautiful, sunny day and spread a red plaid blanket on the sand. The steep Northern California hillsides cascaded into the big blue Pacific Ocean, cradling this small beach that had become my safe cocoon.

"I want to die. I want to die. I want to die," I chanted internally to the rhythm of the waves crashing against the shore.

Snapping out of my trance, I opened my journal. I had to get these thoughts and emotions down somehow. What emerged was a seething letter to God.

"What the hell, God?" I wrote. "I have given you everything I have! After 9/11, I gave up my corporate job to work for peace and compassion, because that's what you called me to do! I gave up my beautiful houseboat on Lake Union in Seattle and moved to California to take a peace-building job—because that's what you called me to do! I took huge risks to heal from cancer naturally, because I heard your messengers loudly and clearly! I'm living like a pauper to serve your will, and yet you still allow cancer to enter my body? You still allow this debilitating depression to keep me from serving you? What am I doing wrong? What memo did I miss, God? Tell me!"

Sobbing, nose running, anger ripping through my body, I jumped to my feet and strode purposefully to the water's edge.

"Dammit God, if you still want me here, you send me a sign right now! Otherwise, I'm done here! I'm done."

At that moment, a sleek, silvery, bottlenose dolphin crested the water directly in front of me and spun in a full circle before ducking back down below the opaque surface of the ocean. Before I had time to feel the full effects of awe welling up within me, a second dolphin broke the surface, spinning joyfully, showering a second mist of salty water before slipping effortlessly back into the sea.

I stood frozen. My mind spoke directly to God: "I'm listening."

As if to punctuate this auspicious moment, God queued a third bottlenose to breach the water and spiral three-hundred-and-sixty degrees before it plunged back down, deep beneath the water's wavy surface.

I was frozen in time. Dried tears streaked salty patterns on my cheeks. My jaw dangled open, agape. God had answered my desperate, frantic prayer *three* times, in glorious splashes of living motion and color.

Stumbling slowly back to my blanket, I rested for countless minutes in stunned silence. I needed to collect myself after witnessing how God showed up on Rodeo Beach dispatching a miraculous trinity of dolphins, calling them into service as prophetic messengers. They had quite capably completed their mission, making my future clear: I am meant to stay in this life and complete my mission of healing physically and mentally, in service to compassion and peace.

A month later, there was no sign of any cancer in my uterus or anywhere else in my body. Yet another Divine miracle had anchored my commitment to stay, heal, and serve.

Emily Hine

ANGEL ENCOUNTER

*T*he road to the ocean was steep and treacherous. My roommate and I called it "Snake Curves."

One evening, as we traveled down this winding road that took us to the Pacific Coast, my roommate, whom I shall call Tessa, shouted, "Slow down, Bonnie! There is an accident ahead!"

As I rounded a corner, I saw a bleeding man lying in the middle of the road. I almost ran over him! Thinking he had been hit by a car, I pulled over. The man was sprawled, face down, on the pavement with his hands tied behind his back.

"Please help me!" he moaned. "I've been shot."

He squeezed Tessa's hand once, and then died. We barely noticed a car that had been parked nearby pulling away.

Another car stopped and we tried CPR, but it was too late. A sheriff's deputy from Malibu questioned us back at the station, in separate rooms, and finally released us early the next morning.

Tessa had worked as a psychic advisor to help law enforcement solve crimes, and she stayed in touch with the sheriff's department. She learned that this apparently had been a drug deal gone wrong. Others had been executed before in the darkness along the Snake Curves. We were both terrified that the car that had left the scene that night belonged to the murderers—and that they had seen my car.

I found myself obsessing about this traumatic experience, unable to sleep and afraid to drive after dark. I was attending acupuncture college at the time, and the nightmarish flashbacks kept me from concentrating on my upcoming exams. Driving the Snake Curves made me especially nervous.

One afternoon, as I was coming home, I spotted a hitchhiker at the bottom of the Curves. The young man had short, curly blond hair. He wore a suit and carried a briefcase. I have never picked up a hitchhiker before or since, but for some reason, I felt compelled to offer this young man a ride. There was something serene and trustworthy about him. As we drove up the winding road, I blurted out what had happened. He listened attentively until we crossed the area where we had found the dying man. Then my passenger looked deeply into my eyes and said, in a soft and reassuring voice, "It's very good that you blessed him with your laying on of hands."

How did he know that? I thought.

A sense of peace and calm came over me.

When we got into the canyon, he gestured to a street at the bottom of a hill, and I let him out there. As I drove off, I turned around. The street was completely empty.

After this experience, my troubling visions stopped. I was able to study, take my exams, and sleep once again. Tessa moved out of the canyon, and I began searching for another house. The one I found was on the same road where I had dropped off the beautiful young man! I truly felt I had been guided there and enjoyed living in that house for many years.

I now have no doubt that I had encountered an angel. The hitchhiker had given me a sign from the spirit world that somehow everything was going to be okay. He had even guided me to my new home.

Unlike Tessa, I am not a psychic. I don't normally see into the energy world. But I now believe that angels can take physical form occasionally, so they can be seen and heard by those of us who do not have that gift—when we are desperately in need of a message.

Dr. Bonnie McLean

SIGNS FROM MOM

*M*om had been my best friend for fifty years, and I was her sole caregiver for her last nine months. I watched her body and mind deteriorate in excruciating increments.

Even though I knew she was dying, her actual transition came with an explosion of grief and sorrow like nothing I had ever experienced. I had been through the deaths of friends and loved ones, and even my stepdad's passing. But this pain was different, so intense I could feel it in my head and body. This was the woman who taught me unconditional love. She had inspired my passions of dancing, cooking, and writing. She was my biggest cheerleader and my source of daily connection and laughter.

I must admit, I felt completely lost for a bit. I have kids, so I went through the motions of daily life for them. Covid had just struck the world, so three of our four children were at home. I knew they were hurting too, missing their grandmother. I couldn't decide whether it was more painful to talk about it or not talk about it. How could I console them when I had this gaping hole in my life where my mom had been?

My belief system told me that my mother wasn't truly "gone," but my instant access to her was different now, and I could not get my head around that.

I started asking for signs that she was still around. Honesty, I wouldn't have noticed any signs during those first few weeks, unless she was standing in front of me waving her hands and saying, "I'm still here!"

But now that I'd asked for them, the signs began to appear. I would find feathers in my path when I went for walks. During morning meditation outside on my deck, I'd glance up and see a huge heart in the clouds. I'd ask for signs when I was in my car, and songs we had both loved would start playing on the radio, even songs that were decades old. Or I'd hear a song with lyrics that were perfect for that moment and what I was feeling.

I was gaining confidence in knowing she was with me, but at the same time, the visceral loss was profound. Questions haunted me. What about those recipes I didn't remember to ask her about? What would I do when I was having a crisis and wanted her nonjudgmental advice? What could take the place of a hug from my mom when I felt scared?

I wallowed in self-pity and grief. Things did not shift until compassion came in.

On the one-year anniversary of my mom's passing, the grief felt fresh and raw again. I was a crying, heaving mess. But then a calm came over me and I remember saying to myself, *Jen, I am so sorry for your loss.* A deeper sensation of compassion and caring accompanied those words. I felt unconditional love. *It was almost as if my mom was there comforting me.*

I felt the deep compassion for myself that I would have felt for a close loved one who was suffering. Yes, it did make me bawl more—but now my tears were a release.

I also had the intuitive hit to ask for another sign, but something more solid this time. I needed to know for sure.

My mom absolutely loved little things. She had more tiny boxes, glasses, and anything else miniature than you can imagine. Any time we were in a store and saw something small or I gave her a gift of a mini mixer magnet for her fridge or any other little gift, it prompted joy and giddiness. I decided to ask her to send me signs of little things, the things she would have loved.

On a walk with my boyfriend, our usual twenty-minute loop around the neighborhood park, I spotted something I'd never noticed before: a little birdhouse in a tree. It was *tiny*, only a few inches tall. I smiled and knew it was a sign. When I tried to find it again, it had vanished. *Thank you, Mom.*

Two years after her death, I hit another grief cycle. Anyone who has been in deep grief knows the process is anything but linear. Other things had gone awry in my life, and I was feeling miserable most of the time. I worried about this. My mom was always so good at getting me through worry and back to laughter and happiness. Now there was nobody to guide me home.

I was out in my backyard and tending to my bunny when a cat came through my yard. My rabbit was terrified of predators, especially cats. I would normally welcome a cat with open arms, but now I wanted to keep this one away.

The cat looked familiar, although I'd never seen it before. I finally realized it was an exact replica of my childhood cat, "Happy," right down to the last detail. Yet I was trying everything I could think of to get this cat to leave my yard, for the rabbit's sake.

I took my bunny inside, since she was showing signs of stress, and comforted her for a while. When I went back outside, Happy was waiting for me. I sank onto a chair on my deck, and she perched directly opposite, staring at me.

I thought, *Good one, Mom. Happy/happiness is staring at me—but will I allow it in or not?*

As the new Happy curled up and fell asleep in a patch of sunlight, I told my mother I appreciated this sign. I would take it to heart. I was going to let happiness back in.

Jenny Mannion

THE SHELF

T he dormitory rooms of Medical Academy Poznań in the communist Poland of 1978 included many students and little furniture. I shared my living space with three other students; we used one bookshelf and one wardrobe. We were allowed to move our furniture around within this tiny space, so we shoved the wardrobe—it was the size of the head of single bed—close to the entry door, hoping to get a bit of privacy from others walking down the busy corridor. I dragged my bed to the space behind the wardrobe, along the wall.

The four of us were studying human anatomy and physiology, biochemistry, pathophysiology, and other medical science subjects. You can imagine the volumes of textbooks we needed to keep in the room. We ran out of bookshelf space on the day we moved in and unpacked. We did not have any floor space left to place another standing bookcase, but my imaginative mind cooked up a solution. I would use the wall over my bed!

I bought a heavy plank of timber, about as wide as a standard textbook— or "bricks" as we called them—and the full length of my bed. With the help of a student who owned a power drill and a screwdriver, we attached hooks to the plank and created a hanging shelf. The other students envied the attractive and cozy little nook I had created for myself, and all my "bricks" had a space off the floor. The shelf also gave my part of the room a little bit of personality.

I spent hours sitting against the wall under that shelf reading, studying, and talking with friends. In time, the contents on the shelf grew, and soon it looked like I had a row of "bricks" above my bed.

I had brought one private and personal item from home: a tiny pillow called "Jasiek" that my grandmother—Babcia Marysia—had made especially for me. With my head nestled on Jasiek, in my private nook, I felt cozy and less homesick.

The university courses were intensive. All of us studied for many exams, completed multiple assignments, and prepared for our practical exercises. We often did our schoolwork until late at night.

After one long day, I collapsed in my bed at midnight and fell asleep immediately. Very soon after, I heard a voice calling.

"Wake up! Wake up! Joanna, wake up!"

I was so exhausted, I tried to stay asleep. But the voice was insistent.

"Joanna, wake up! Wake up now!"

When I again failed to rouse myself, the voice called again:

"Sit up now! Look out the window. The sun is up and shining. Get up now!"

Finally, I sat up and opened my eyes. I saw a surprisingly bright and shiny day outside, even though that window faced the brick wall of another building and never seemed to let in any light.

Then one side of my bookshelf crashed down.

The edge of the heavy plank landed exactly in the middle of my little pillow, where my head had been just seconds earlier. In shock, I looked at the window and saw that the beautiful, sunny day had somehow disappeared. It was still dark, the middle of the night. My three roommates slept soundly.

For a moment, I considered pulling my Jasiek out from under the shelf and the chaos of books that had fallen on top of it, but I was too tired to expend that much effort. Instead, I quietly lay down on the bed space that was left and went back to sleep.

When I opened my eyes next, I heard commotion and saw several of my colleagues standing around my bed.

"You are lucky!" I heard them exclaiming.

"That could have killed you."

"The edge of that shelf could have fractured your skull!"

I sat up, suddenly remembering what had happened. Half of the dent from where my head had rested was still visible on my little pillow. I looked out the window and saw the brick wall, just a few meters away. Even though the sun was up now, it would never shine through this window.

But for me, it had.

"Thank you," I whispered to whatever had saved my life.

Who placed the beautiful, shiny picture in front of my eyes that cut through my exhausted slumber? Who shouted the warning words in my mind to wake me up?

It might have been my guardian angel, my departed grandfather, my spiritual father, my higher self, or some cosmic protector. Perhaps, one day, I'll get to know.

For now, I am simply grateful for the intervention. Something or someone had preserved my health and saved my life with a shout and a ray of sunshine, just at the right moment.

Joanna Kazmirowicz

IT'S TIME TO BUY A HOUSE

*H*ouses have arrived in my life with illusory ease. Standing proudly, my future homes would beam signals at my consciousness and open their doorways of possibility, drawing me in. An incessant inner voice, with mouse-like hurriedness and cat-like defiance, would begin its niggling: *Come on, come on... There's no time to waste. Start looking now!*

The words would feverishly circle my waking mind, chasing their tails each morning. I knew the game was once again in play, without warning and without question. When the time came to make my move, a parade of pointers would arise like little breadcrumbs, guiding me home. Of that, I could be certain.

It had been that way my whole life. Every house had its language, and each had called for me in its own, distinct voice. When I'd purchased a home, it was because of an instantaneous knowing, a concrete flash of insight, as unshakable as the foundations upon which they stood. Surprisingly, the same unspoken truth showed up when I rented.

Having left my husband on the dawn of my thirtieth year, I stepped out into the big, wide world of rentals, a figurative virgin. "I really want to paint a wall purple!" I giddily blurted to my friend, who rode shotgun as we cruised, all four windows down, around the bayside suburbs of Melbourne. We were on the hunt for my next abode—just two single gals, soaking up the fertile, springtime vibes that wafted in on the salty scent of new beginnings.

I was doing everything I'd been warned not to: divorcing, selling, moving away, renting. And now I had the strangest urge to paint something purple, a color I scarcely liked!

"You can't do that," my friend casually threw back my way as I eased the car into the last viewing on this weekend's search. "You're renting now."

Taken aback by her dose of reality, I scooped up my burst bubble of creative freedom and ambled, less certain, toward the gated entrance. Things were changing rapidly in so many ways. Singledom had required so many unforeseen adjustments. And now I felt glum to realize I'd be forbidden to paint a wall that bruisy, berry color that filled me with a sense of excitement and liberation.

The top-floor studio that rose in front of me was not completely unfamiliar. I'd fantasized about married life within its walls some years ago, when summer days would have us driving past this building from our suburban backyard to the seaside, our car loaded with friends. I eyed the metal numbers on the slatted fence as we entered. This was 555 Main Street. The available space was Unit 11. Eleven had been my marker since a teen, when I would routinely wake up at 11:11 p.m. and notice it flash on clocks during the day. It was my sign to pay attention. Coupled with triple digits, my life was a jackpot of symbology. Intuitively, I sensed a little halo of gold go "ding."

Inviting us safely in was a private, internal stairwell, snugged into the rear of the courtyard. As we gathered in the foyer, I turned to follow the agent upstairs and quietly gasped. The towering backdrop of the two-story staircase was a single, lavender wall flanked by its white sisters.

I turned to my friend and smirked, "Well, there's my purple wall, and I didn't have to do a thing!"

I moved in the following week.

But time passed, more things changed, and I was again hearing the voices telling me to land—and I wasn't even looking for a house! I was embarking on another new chapter with a new man and a new perspective. We'd set sail on the tarred inland causeways of Australia from the shorelines of Melbourne, caravan in tow and destination unknown. We planned to live as gypsies for the conceivable future and love every gilded moment of it. This hammering voice in my head was not expected, and to be honest, not welcome! With no conscious longing to settle down anywhere right now, why was I being instructed to find a home?

Night after night, I awoke with its words prodding at me. The dream-like state hung thick as I readied myself, fading during the day but at the new dawn, it would be back, inexplicably rousing. It was relentless, and I began to submit.

Although we hadn't been talking about any need to nest, I soon announced to my partner it was time to look for a house. He knew well enough that my crazy often turned into incredible, and the track record on my house instincts so far had served me well, so he jumped aboard this next adventure without protest.

We focused our search within a carefully curated region we had scoped in our travels: Northern New South Wales, from Bellingen to Byron Bay. With its lush lands rising, endless beaches crashing, and temperate, tropical weather ready to bask and bathe you, this area was a sweet, earthy, Australian heaven. Aside from our dotted line border, we were otherwise uncontained, like fossicking for gold in the Atlantic. If something fell within budget, it was a prospect, a claim of potential return, forcing us to choose with our hearts and hearts alone.

Winding down the road to our second stakeout for the day, outside a town we'd never visited, verdant rainforest greeted us—as I had begun to envision it would when we found the right home. The roads in had been all tarmac and potholes, with 360-degree farmland vistas beautifully patchworked by nature. It wasn't exactly as my visionary signs had indicated in the weeks leading up to this road trip—but now, tingles of expectation grew as I melded into the natural surroundings. The dirt road, unbreathed air, and shades of green foliage enveloped my senses. An ease and familiarity overcame me.

Pausing momentarily at the gate flung wide—a quintessential welcoming token to enter any country property—my partner gave me a big, fat, Cheshire-cat grin.

"This is our home," he purred, licking his paws.

"Darling, perhaps leave the negotiating to me, hey!" I quipped as we rolled on in. His face was unmistakably beaming, "Take my money, take all my money."

A giant-of-a-man greeted us, the same man whose hands had built this well-worn, verandah-cloaked homestead some forty years earlier. Although an imposing figure, he was endearing. I felt an instant peace in his presence. There seemed to be no hiding from him as he began interviewing us to determine our credentials as contending custodians of his beloved timber temple. I'd never been through such an experience before. We were the sales pitch!

His level of ownership was unexpected but signaled to me that his values were in alignment with our own. Having heard the answers he was quietly seeking, he generously offered us a weekend stay in his big, empty house. There was no electricity, but he would leave some wood for the fire, and we'd have time to get a feel for the place. Buying a house is a big deal. Buying a house when you had no intention, in a place you know nearly nothing about, is even bigger. We felt his offer was a gracious demonstration that there was more for us to explore.

Within weeks, we were back at the gate, now closed but willing us to unlatch it and welcome ourselves in. A huge decision hung on the next two days, and although it would have taken an enormous protest to convince my husband that this was not our next home, I needed further validation that it was the right step forward. It had been me, after all, with the nagging thoughts, the cat-and-mouse game in play, and it was a wild leap of faith to move into this isolated place, so far away from friends and family.

Suddenly, it seemed a snowball of significance was precipitously poised to begin rolling. I asked the universe for a quick sign and glanced over to the odometer. Five-five-five. I gulped and smiled as the magical number disappeared on our roll down the driveway.

This would not be the only sign this weekend, but it set a tone. We camped out inside this quiet space with cathedral ceilings that could have spoken volumes. It felt old and lived in and loved and deserted, all at once. It seemed ready for someone new to inhabit its walls and create stories for the next forty years. As I made my way upstairs to meditate in one of the vast rooms, my husband ventured out, Huckleberry Finn-like, to roam the land.

In meditation, I was taken into the yard behind the house, beyond the rickety stairs but before the orchard of peaches and pears, where a vortex of energy arose from the land. A vision of a chair-sized piece of rose quartz crystal appeared in the center point as people gathered around. I felt the sun streaming down with importance and life force. In the moments after meditation, I wrote to my guides and received this message: *Be still in the silence this Divine location offers your soul. You have found your sanctuary. Your spiritual birthplace.*

My husband turned up some time later, soaked from head to foot, his Cheshire smile returned. He had been coaxed into exploring the crystalline creek that bordered the property and had trekked from one end to the other, only to discover it was much deeper in some places. He told me a white frog had been following him with seeming intention as he moved downstream. We'd never heard of white frogs and took delight in something so unique making this place its home.

As we lazed on the back deck in the setting sun, I saw an apparition of a close friend from Melbourne walking barefoot on the grass, free and happy. Next, a small being arrived and I saw future visions of this star-friend sitting by my side on the verandah's edge, discussing all manner of worldly wisdom. Except in meditative states, it was not common for me to see visions so freely. I could hardly believe my eyes. Yet these visions had such presence that it was impossible not to trust in the seeing.

With the car almost packed after a glorious weekend, I dashed over to the patch of grass where the vortex of energy had appeared in my meditation. I stood, arms out, soaking in the mountainous landscape before me. I took a snapshot with my mind of what might one day become our own. Closing my eyes, I took myself into a moment of meditation and immediately felt my legs sink, knee deep, into the soil. This was something I'd never experienced. My legs had become solid tree trunks, embedded and unmoving. I stayed in this state until I opened my eyes again and could walk away freely.

I pleaded for one final sign before I went to sleep that night. Although everything felt right and the signs all pointed to yes, this purchase wasn't just a house but a frightfully drastic, albeit thrilling, change to our previous way of life. The decision needed to be rock solid. I'd have no quick way to make an about-turn if I changed my mind.

I awoke the next morning to visions of energetic pyramids flashing simultaneously over the house and vortex. This seemed an amazing indication of the power this place held for me personally. But another sign emerged that night that would seal the deal. As we prepared for bed, there on our bedroom wall, we spotted a frog. A white frog. A sign of transition and spiritual evolution. Ribbit, ribbit, ribbit.

We rented out our new home as we continued to indulge our wanderlust for a while, unsure of when and why we needed to be there but entrusting that all would become clear in time. And when it was time, this house not only spoke but screamed for my return. Nothing could have stopped us from getting back there the second we needed to.

Life flowed, with steps rising and blocks dissolving in unison. It became the epitome of Divine timing: effortlessness, grace, speed, and simplicity, when your wildest imaginings become intrinsic knowings, and nothing but trust lights your path.

Signs and synchronicity are symbiotic. The signs get you there, and the synchronicity keeps you going.

Hayley Barkla

THE BUTTERFLIES AND
THE SWALLOWS

I n the Western Cape of South Africa, the heat can be relentless. Taking a walk before the sun rose higher and the heat increased, I followed the dirt road, being careful of where I stepped. In this part of the world, it's important to stay on the alert for any footprints that might indicate wild animals prowling around. I saw several snakeskins, but none was fresh-looking enough to mean that the owner was nearby. I also knew that I had to be careful not to pass any piles of cow dung, as they were sometimes puff-adders in disguise.

Craving the serenity of the reservoir, I strolled along the water's edge enjoying the sound of nature: chirping crickets, singing birds, and buzzing insects. The natural sound effects made the reservoir seem still and calm. The air was thick with a haughty smell of flowering shrubs and the ground vegetation releasing the dew of the morning.

Everything was so colorful, except for the dusty, gray road. Ahead of me, I saw a blanket of lovely yellow. *What could this be?* I wondered. As I walked closer, the blanket suddenly rose into the air. It was a swarm of yellow butterflies of all sizes, from as tiny as my fingernail to as long as my ring finger.

I passed by—but then I realized the butterflies were coming with me! They flew all around me, as if they were dancing and showing off. The moment was breathtaking. I was heading for a shady part of the road where I could sit next to a small creek to cool off. The area was full of beautiful purple and blue flowers that reminded me of bluebells, but much larger.

My plan was to meditate sitting on a tiny bridge where the air was cooled by the running water below and the ants didn't venture. There was a lovely serenity in the scent of the flowers there. The butterflies might enjoy it ...

Suddenly, I noticed that the swarm had stopped as if it had come to a glass wall. The butterflies were on one side of this invisible division, and I was on the other. Why had they stopped? There was no shade there and nothing around indicating that the road was different or changed. I walked a few moments without them, but then I got a strange, gut feeling that it was not safe to go further.

On the left side of the road was an opening to a cave, which people had told me was deep and long. Sometimes, they said, wild animals sheltered there. A week earlier I had seen, in the mud near the cave, the footprints of a mature leopard and smaller prints from a cub. The local people believed the big cats had since returned to higher ground.

After mulling things over, I realized that the butterflies and my gut feeling were saying the same thing: It was not safe to continue. I turned and walked back. The moment I came to where they had stopped, they all swarmed around me again and walked with me to my car. Then they sat again on the road. I had a strong feeling of protection and gratitude.

A week later, I was sitting on a balcony in another location when I was swarmed again—this time by a huge flock of swallows. I stood up and went to the banister and they flew all around me in waves, showing their underbellies. Their feathers were blue and violet. It was exhilarating to be once again surrounded by all this beauty. The birds brought to my mind the swarm of butterflies.

Those two moments lifted me up emotionally. Both left me with a feeling of gratitude and love. But were they a sign?

I believe the truth they brought was about being interconnected, as I had felt connected to both the butterflies and the swallows. We are all interconnected within the tapestry of life. All living things—every insect, animal, flower, tree, human, and all other beings that are around us, even though we do not see them—are us, and we are them.

We are all one, and life is precious beyond understanding.

Agustina Thorgilsson

A STRANGER'S DOG

*T*he pandemic affected everybody in diverse ways. The lives of so many turned upside down into an abyss of loss, pain, and transformation.

For much of 2020, we were kept in quarantine, isolated, struggling to understand this new situation. In my solitary confinement, trying not to catch this still-deadly virus, I stayed connected through phone conversations and texts, but I was often alone with only prayer to keep me company.

My family and friends lived in different states and boroughs. My eighty-six-year-old sister Lillian and her husband, who lived in the Bronx, and my younger brother living near the Canadian border, stayed in close contact. We kept reassuring each other that we were being careful and doing our best to stay safe from Covid.

But on the morning of April 2, 2020, my sister's husband informed me that the virus had caught Lillian. She was in an intensive care unit. As he spoke, my heart kept saying, *No, this is a dream! This isn't happening!*

I needed to see her. All hospitals were still on strict lockdown, with no visitors allowed. In the beginning of the pandemic, even family members were forbidden to enter the hospitals—only the patients and the heavily-garbed doctors and nurses could walk inside.

But she was in a hospital just twenty-five blocks from where I live in Manhattan, and I began walking there. My plan was to find a way to sneak in and visit Lillian. I was shocked to find the hospital was like a fortress. Standing at the guarded entrance, I realized that I might never see my sister ever again. Because of her age and health issues, she might never get out of this hospital—and I couldn't get in.

Numb, I trod the twenty-five blocks back to my apartment through desolate streets, passing shuttered stores. The barren avenues made New York feel like a different planet. Everything was surreal. Suddenly, I couldn't stop the sea of tears. I tried to scream, "Why? Why God?" but no sound would come out. The only thing that felt real was my love for my sister and for God.

Back at my apartment, anger, rage, and sadness threatened to pull me under. The world was out of control. Lillian had stayed homebound, trying to hide from the killer disease, and she had caught it anyway. The idea that she was fighting this alone, without family for support, was more than I could bear.

The doctors and nurses became the angels in my daydreams...and a glimpse of gratitude would come into my heart, knowing that they cared. I began to call the hospital daily. For many days, no one in the intensive care unit would pick up the phone. To keep myself sane, I kept saying, "I have no control over this. Someone will eventually pick up." I deeply prayed for her recovery and handed everything over to Divine power.

Two weeks later, a nurse startled me by answering the phone. She was able to tell me that Lillian was still in critical condition and on a ventilator. She allowed me to speak to the doctor in charge. I pleaded with him to let me see her via Facetime. Video chatting wasn't allowed during the height of the pandemic, but he was a compassionate doctor, and he made an exception for me. I am forever indebted to him for this act of mercy.

Though it was deeply painful to see my sister looking so weak and helpless, I had the chance to tell her that we loved her. I pleaded for her to pull through, reminding her that she had always been strong. She'd survived cancer and heart attacks. I said we were looking forward to her recovering and coming home. But, because I could see that she was gravely ill, I also let her know that, if she felt she wanted to move on, it was okay to surrender to the Divine.

In my heart, I kept hoping and praying that she would somehow pull through. But on April 16, dear Lilly made her transition.

For a time, guilt overwhelmed me. I couldn't sleep or eat, and I sank into a deep depression. I wondered, *Could I have done more?* But I knew I'd tried everything I could in this horrible situation.

What got me through was a phrase I started repeating during this dark time: "I surrender, and I am not in control." As I faced each day, moment by moment, breath by breath, this mantra kept bringing me back to a place of solace.

Losing a loved one is never easy, but somehow during this pandemic, it was even more agonizing. Not being able to comfort my sibling as she faced death made my grief sharper, and I know other families experienced this as well. I tried to cling to a sense of inner peace, feeling that my sister was still being taken care of and so was I. It was time to "let go and let God," to trust whatever was unfolding.

I began to feel that my sister was trying to make a connection by gifting me small signs as I leaned into my sorrow. On the first anniversary of her transition, the interwoven dance of sadness and alignment began with a more dramatic sign.

Though I wanted to stay in bed under the covers, I felt compelled to go to Central Park. I made myself get up, get ready, and leave the apartment. Then I slowly made my way to the West 79th Street entrance.

I usually entered at a different spot, but intuition was leading me, so I followed it. The brisk and cloudy day reflected my innermost feelings as I strode alone, asking myself why this pandemic had to come and take my sister. I had no answers.

I remembered growing up with Lillian, our fun times, our sweet and painful times. I could hear her hearty laugh and smell her delicious cooking. I thought of how she loved plants and how we saw life and spirituality so differently. The sadness each time I remembered she was no longer here shattered me.

In the middle of the park, I came across two frisky squirrels chasing each other. They stopped to look at me and slowly scampered closer in an inquisitive way. When I said hello, they raced around my legs, shook their fluffy tails, and scrambled up a tree. Suddenly, I felt their joy of being high above the ground.

Huge, grayish rocks loomed nearby and knew I needed to sit on top of them. The climb was steep, and I struggled to get to the summit, but the view made it worthwhile. *Wow! My own little oasis.* I could see every corner of the park from there with the sacredness of Mother Nature all around me.

I watched people strolling past and wondered if any of them were also grieving someone they lost to Covid. So many people died during that time.

I thanked the rocks for helping me to get grounded. I told them that I felt I was falling apart and needed their help. I lay down and felt my heartbeat connecting with their energy. Then I sat up and started to cry again.

A lady walked by, followed by her cute Jack Russell terrier, a tiny white dog with black and brown markings. Suddenly, the dog stopped and looked back. He glanced up and spotted me sitting on the rocks.

In a flash, the terrier darted away from its owner and sprinted up the rocks, landing in my lap! His arrival almost knocked me down. I clutched his furry body as he looked up at me with soulful, caramel-colored eyes, as if he knew me. I was stunned by the sudden upswell of love I felt from this adorable dog, whom I'd never met before. I felt my heart being cracked wider.

A mixture of sadness and profound joy overcame me as his soft pink tongue licked my tears away.

The owner waited patiently for her dog. She didn't try to call him back. It was as if she knew this perfect stranger needed the blessing of the little creature's Divine love, and he was on a mission to comfort my aching heart.

Each time I think of this sacred moment, my heart melts, filling me with warmth and unconditional love. It reminds me that I'm being looked after and guided and that my sister is also protected on the other side. I still can't believe that this magical moment happened, but it did. My angelic intervention came from a small, affectionate dog, and that was the beginning of my healing.

There is so much more to loss, tragedy, and life than I can ever comprehend. At the most unexpected times, sacred moments show up. They will always show up. That faith is an anchor.

The little dog was my sign that the Divine is all around me and those I love and will be forever.

Maryann Sussoni

ONE FINAL GIFT

first saw the Mother Tree across the wide field that was my new back yard. A majestic Live Oak, she had, like many of her kind, one long, lower branch emerging from her trunk, stretching twenty-five or thirty feet into the surrounding meadow. To me, that branch always looked like a long arm reaching out to embrace the earth, to shelter and protect the dozens of small saplings growing at her feet. She was the image of abundance with her rich crown above and her plentiful progeny below. The limb seemed to make a gesture of giving, of bestowing, as if she were sprinkling blessings on the ground below her.

The long branch also made the tree seem unstable. Indeed, when we met, she was already leaning. A deluge, the souvenir of a tropical storm, had loosened the grasp of her roots in the sandy Florida soil.

As we began the process of settling into our new home, my dog Jesse and I explored the back acreage. The spacious open areas were densely packed with the various wildflowers that sprang up between mowings. A small pond in the back corner had become a hang-out spot for snakes, otters, turtles, and even gators. Whistling ducks had found a cavity in the branches of an old snag and built a nest there. The back edge of the property was wild growth, full of ferns, vines, and briars, impassable to human feet.

Wherever we wound up on our wanderings, we always began them by visiting the Mother Tree. The long branch was just a little taller than me, and I would ask permission to come into her space and touch it. She always granted me that opportunity. I would reach up and hug her with my hands. I traced her bark delicately with my fingers. It was rough with lichens and small tufts of moss growing in the craggy furrows.

The tree was perhaps seventy-five to eighty years old and had no doubt experienced a great deal in that time. I thought of the thousands of migrating songbirds who had rested on her branches along their journey. Generations of squirrels and clutches of avian babies had found a home in her boughs. She had witnessed the changing landscape in the near distance, which had shifted from a natural area to an orange grove, then to a small goat farm, and now to a home along a bustling street.

Though there were forty or more trees on the property, of several species, I knew immediately she was the Mother Tree.

I started each morning, while Jesse explored the back areas, by greeting and sharing a loving moment with the Mother Tree. Her energy was beautiful. She was nurturing, an island of loving kindness nestled amidst the harshness of passing sirens and other chaos. I treasured greeting the day in her presence.

Then one day, it happened. Another tropical storm passed through. I was working about two miles away and watched in awe as the skies opened and the rain pounded down for hours. I had never seen such a dense downpour. My usual short drive home was long and slow that night as the ditches on either side had swollen and overflowed into the street, with more than seven inches of rain that day.

I went to bed that night, as I did many times in that house, wondering if the flood waters would seep under the doorway and into my living space. We were spared. The same was not true for the Mother Tree.

When the morning came, I stepped outside into a surprisingly calm and sunny day. Water stood ankle deep in many places in the yard, but piles of leaves and twigs in the road showed the floodwaters were already beginning to recede. I turned to look toward the back, and there I saw my friend, the Mother Tree, sprawled across the lawn.

The huge amount of water had further loosened her roots and she had tipped too far; her mighty weight had come crashing down to rest on the earth. She was probably thirty-five to forty feet long, stretched out.

I walked now among her branches, seeing remnants of all the life she had sheltered: air plants, mosses, a nest. Her beautiful crown, now horizontal, was still way over my head. As I returned to the house, I hoped my landlord would just let the tree stay there and grow horizontally. Sometimes folks did that.

But soon there was a commotion in the back yard and a swarm of men with chain saws began the huge job of dismantling her branches. I plugged my ears the best I could and put on music, trying to drown out the saws and the sounds of the men. While they celebrated their efficient teamwork, inside the house, I wept.

That evening, after the men had dispersed and the saws were silenced, I walked back to visit the Mother Tree, now in pieces. I had loved this tree so much, and now she was gone. I stepped over logs and around limbs until I got to the stump.

I gasped when I saw it. On the huge, round scar where she had been cut, her sap had formed the shape of a heart.

She loved us, too.

She held no bitterness toward those who had cut her down. It was her time. Generations of giving her gifts of oxygen, homes, and food were now ended.

And in her last moments, she found a way to give us one last gift.

Her best.

Her love.

Anne Cederberg

MY CRYSTAL ANGEL

a year after my mother passed away, I knew it was time to end my relationship. We had mirrored each other's grief—he had lost his mom as well—but now our shared pain felt suffocating. It was time to start fresh. It might be time to pursue my dream of hosting wellness retreats in Jamaica, where I was born. I also yearned for a connection to my ancestry.

In the city of Negril, I met a massage therapist who told me he also wanted to host healing retreats! He described his home, which was carved out of the side of a mountain with its own mountain spring, as a magical space for people to heal. I was excited about what seemed to be a divine business connection. We shared our vision for what these retreats would entail and our love for the healing arts. We began the thought process of developing a new venture. He invited me to visit his home, so I could get a feel of the space and to connect our vision.

By chance, a few days before I was to leave, I met a man on the beach in front of my bungalow. His strong, relaxed, protective energy made me feel connected to him. We spent hours talking and sharing life stories. He showed me his quartz crystal, which was a cherished gift from a friend in Switzerland.

He had the crystal wrapped in white cloth; once it was unwrapped, it grabbed the sunlight and dispersed every color in its prism: blues, purples, pink. The stone was gorgeous and illuminating. I felt warm in its presence.

He said he considered it a powerful talisman and even believed it to be a living entity. "It has saved me countless times," he said.

My new friend from the beach stopped by every morning. He had become my travel guide in the Westmoreland parish of Jamaica, introducing me to all the magical caves, rivers, and blue holes in the area.

The morning when I was to leave for the massage therapist's mountain house, he insisted he go up the mountain with me. I welcomed his company. I had come to trust his insights, and I was certain my potential business partner would, too.

We set off on our journey to Sheffield, the small village in a valley at the foot of the mountain, and then made our way up. The mountain house was pure magnificence: lush, green, fresh, Edenic. The massage therapist had not exaggerated when he described his home; this place was godly. When we arrived, I introduced my guide to our host, who welcomed him. We hung out in his open-air living space, enjoying the view of treetops, hills, and birds. The fragrant air was enchanting. This would be a wonderful site for a retreat.

We cooked, broke bread together, and discussed our vision for creating the perfect space for visitors to detoxify and reclaim themselves. The next day, I bathed in the mountain spring, walked the grounds, and smelled the wild, exotic flowers. I harvested an armful of mangoes, soursop, and guavas, envisioning bringing people to this garden of wellness. I went to bed that night in full gratitude, feeling aligned with this manifestation yet keeping my heart detached from the outcome.

The following morning, my guide woke me.

"You need to pack now and get ready to leave," he said in a calm whisper. "This man means you no good."

I stared at him; time stood still as I felt as if I had stepped into an alternate reality.

"But why? Did I miss something since last night?" I asked.

"We need to go."

As I got dressed, I could hear the massage therapist barking loudly in his Jamaican patois, "Who does she think she is, bringing another man into my house!"

He shouted at my guide, "I am going to kill the both of you!"

When I left the bedroom carrying my packed bag, I could see our host screaming and waving a cutlass.

My guide pressed his cherished crystal into my right palm and said, "Hold it and keep walking until you are at the bottom of the mountain."

He repeated, "Hold the crystal."

He guarded my back as I made my descent down the mountain. I held tight to the crystal, which had turned onyx black. I felt overwhelmingly calm. The negative energy was so heightened it felt as if a volcano had erupted and was spewing hot lava behind me, yet I felt safe. I held tight to the crystal, now black as tar, and I prayed earnestly.

As I descended away from the chaos, the black within the crystal began to change to emerald green, beginning at the crown. By the time I reached the bottom of the mountain, the massage therapist and his rage were far behind me, and the crystal was completely clear.

Had this crystal absorbed all the negative energy that was directed at me? I only knew that holding it had helped me feel calm, safe, and Divinely protected.

My guide was minutes behind me, and he also arrived safely at the bottom of the mountain. He had never seemed flustered by any of the chaos. He'd accompanied me up the mountain and back down as if he was assigned to the task.

He and the crystal were one, and he was already imbued with its Divine power. After all, he did say the crystal had saved him numerous times. And now it had saved me.

Khepera Sek Km

DOLPHIN HEART

The *Shaktima* moved through the emerald waters of the Gulf of Mexico like a bird in flight. Her sails steered us towards the invisible shore we had left at sunrise. The offshore winds had been perfect for a cruise far into the gulf, and now Capitan Petter had turned her about.

Our vessel was zigzagging her way back when we saw the pod of jumping dolphins.

All our eyes were fixated on the splashes ahead. The dolphins were taking turns making high jumps, spiraling, and diving as they flicked their tails. Amongst all the exuberant joy, two dolphins facing each other jumped high into the air and, like synchronized swimmers, they turned their bodies slightly toward the water.

Their shining bluish gray backs were outlining a heart. Their tails came together into a point close to the water, their backs bent into a circle with their heads smack in the center, pointed at their tails. The image froze. Time stopped with the clear, blue sky shining in a perfect heart shape, outlined by the pink bellies of the dolphins.

We were as excited as the dolphins as we took it all in. I breathed the image—which I had seen in my meditation only a few months back—into my entire body. It was a dolphin heart I was drawing, a knowingness of their message to live in love and birth in love. Love is the perfect fluid! Warm, conducive, comfortable, accepting, flexible, enduring, compassionate, and potent—love was what the dolphins were telling me to teach about!

As a birth doula, love is not always easy to blend into the birth scene. It has been easier to share about water or swimming with dolphins. What a surprise it is to simply say, Love is the perfect fluid! I needed this dolphin sign to manifest the message into the real, three-dimensional world. I needed to see it first in my mind's eye, and then to draw it, and then experience it. Now it had come alive in me, where it could generate a hope and firm belief that it is possible to manifest.

Love and the joy of dolphins can be part of family births.

Love is the wild dolphin's sign to deliver a new generation of beings from the heart of the sacred womb.

Love is the dolphin's message, and you are to pass it on into the world.

I understood all that in the everlasting instant while I witnessed my drawing coming to life.

They had more to say: *Look at us, learn from us, be like us!*

Then I understood that it is not so much about being *with* dolphins, it is about being *like* dolphins.

In deep gratitude for the language of signs, their manifestation, and what the dolphins had brought into being, I pray that this fluid, magical substance continues to permeate all births and beyond, in waves of love.

Marina Alzugaray

DIVINE'S WAY OF TOUCH

The signs started slowly and subtly, but they carried an energy that ignited my curiosity. Hands were everywhere! I saw hands on magazine and book covers and people walking while holding hands. I heard about hand surgeries, gardening hands, and babies' hands. It seems like wherever I was, hands were catching my attention.

I particularly remember a man who came up to me at the farmers market and took off his gloves to help me carry some bird seed to my car. A tattoo on his hand said, "Focus." That was *the* spectacle that I needed. I decided to pay close attention to this sign.

For the next ten days, the energy subsided, but I remained more "focused" on what my hands were doing and what I was doing with them.

Then, one sunny, hot afternoon, my nervous system went haywire. I had a syncope episode, meaning I lost consciousness and fell flat onto the desert ground. When I regained my wits, I realized I had fallen into a cactus and my hand was covered in cactus thorns. My injuries kept me from my busy life. I slowly learned there was much more going on with my nervous system than just a simple "fight or flight" reaction, or even dehydration. I had a chronic condition that was getting more serious, and I needed medical attention.

Doctor appointments, bloodwork, MRI, scans, endless questions, and no concrete answers from the medical community followed. These days left me saddened and on my own. Searching for answers, curious about my healing and increasingly desperate, I remembered the countless days of seeing hands. I decided to return my focus to mine.

I started to look at the wounds and infection from the cactus. I made it my daily mission to place my hands in prayer position and bring my lips to them, for solace and to show my gratitude. I was grateful I hadn't been hurt more severely. I could still use my hands to cook, clean, and take care of myself. And I was relieved to know that the wounds would heal in time.

Because my nervous system needed time to reintegrate, I spent my days homebound, in and out of sleep cycles. I now had time to receive messages and decipher them. I was being prepared for a wonderful gift.

The signs started again and came consistently for seven days, during a nap or during sleep. They seemed to build on one another. The first night there was a sparkle of light and the second night, I saw fingers. The third night was the palm of a hand, the fourth night the entire hand, and on the fifth night, I saw two infinity signs (one on my ring finger and one on my middle finger). On the sixth night, the word *proprioception* appeared on the back side of my hand in a vision. And on the seventh night, the letters *JSJ* showed up on my palm.

I was perplexed but also in awe. As my curiosity intensified, I became determined to understand these messages. I had no idea where to begin, but I was very sure of something: My excitement and motivation were exactly what I needed to overcome barriers to this new health challenge.

I didn't need to search too far. Spirit was guiding and communicating with me along the way. Interestingly, a few days later, I was listening to a lecture on the computer where someone was explaining an ancient energy practice called Jin Shin Jyutsu, which is a healing modality that uses the hands to balance the body and mind. It is a practice that redirects the body and nervous system to a more coherent state through proprioception.

That's it! I thought. The letters on my hand in the vision were prompting me to learn this creative and profound art called Jin Shin Jyutsu.

I began immediately. The results were astonishing. I was able to use this practice to gently give my body and nervous system the etheric nourishment and touch they needed. The results gave me the confidence to commit to the practice.

Each day, I focused on a symptom and gained more clarity about energy and moving it through the body. The visions and signs had connected me to the universal intelligence that serves all.

Tamara Knox

HEALING WITH CRYSTALS

*W*orking on a keyboard for long hours every day had taken a toll on my hands and wrists. I had developed carpal tunnel syndrome so extreme that shooting pains in my hands began awakening me at night. Yet I postponed the surgery that could have stopped my pain. I'd had surgery for other things, but I strongly felt that surgery on my wrists and tendons was not going to be good for me. I couldn't bring myself to have the procedure.

After several months of misery, I mentioned my wrist problems to my mother-in-law. She was not only a friend, but a trusted mentor for me—and she said something surprising.

"I think I know someone who can help you."

She said that her group at Unity Church (a metaphysical church) had hosted a speaker the prior week who was a chiropractor who also did energy work and used crystals for healing. She said he had spoken at length about how crystal therapy could help some people avoid more invasive treatments.

I thought, *Hmmm, this is interesting.* I finally admitted to someone that I've got a medical problem, and the universe put in front of me exactly what I was looking for: non-surgical therapy for my ailment. *What a coincidence ...*

I had been fascinated by energy healing for a while and I deeply wanted to have the power to help someone, even in a small way.

Our guides often won't give us all the information we need at once. They hand it to us in digestible amounts, a chapter at a time, sometimes a sentence at a time. We just must trust that everything we learn is leading to an important revelation about our role in the world.

I made an appointment with the chiropractor, telling him I did not want any chiropractic treatments—just crystal healing therapy for carpal tunnel syndrome.

The day for my appointment came and I met the chiropractor. He was young, probably under thirty, and he seemed excited that I wanted to try this unconventional therapy. First, he made me watch a video about homeopathic therapies that reminded me that healing came with no guarantees, but it was important to be open and receptive to anything that might happen.

I prepared myself and set the intention that I would receive healing on all levels to resolve my carpal tunnel and any other issues that needed healing or attunement at this time, for my highest good always.

His therapy room was white and peaceful, more like a fancy massage spa than a treatment room. It had a spiritual rather than clinical feel. A table held some mechanical chiropractic tools, but the doctor went instead to a good-size crystal, about eight inches long, which was taped or attached to a longer handle. The chiropractor started to move the crystal in a circular pattern around my wrists and hands, from my elbows down to my fingertips.

As he worked, my pain disappeared.

We were chatting about crystals. I told him that people had just started giving me crystals about six months ago.

"I get them as gifts, but I don't know what to do with them."

"That's probably a sign that you should be working with them," he said. "It's all about intention. Crystals can help people heal. If people only knew the power of crystals, the world could be transformed into a better place."

"But I don't know how to work with them."

"Anyone can do this," he said. "The crystals heal when you use intention and just make a slight movement over the areas that need healing."

He suggested that I lie back on the massage table. He put on some spiritual music and went into the other room. Suddenly, to my amazement, I saw the largest orb of light that I've ever seen, before or since. This huge, golden, bubbly ball of light began bouncing up and down in an upper corner of the room. I felt it come into the room before I saw it, because it carried a huge, loving presence. The ball of golden light was three to four feet across, and it seemed to hang from the ceiling, showering me with light and with love. I immediately felt that an angel or other spiritual being inhabited this orb. It had come to give me an attunement and to show me beyond question that I was being healed. The angel seemed to convey that Spirit was aware of my needs and was showing me the next crucial step on my journey.

I realized that crystals were going to be an important part of this journey and that I was to use them for my benefit and to help others.

When the chiropractor returned, he asked me how I felt. I told him my pain had disappeared. Then I shared with him that I could see a huge orb of golden light. It was still there, although he couldn't see it.

I went home and immediately pulled out my small collection of crystals. I empowered one of the crystals with an intention for healing, as my chiropractor had suggested. That first attunement with the large crystal kept my carpal tunnel at bay for about a week; when the pain returned, I was prepared. I had my little healing crystal at the ready.

I did movements with the crystal over my wrists, hands, and fingers, as the chiropractor had instructed—and just like before, the pain vanished. At first, I had to repeat this process several times a week, and then every other week, and then once a month. After about six months, I realized I no longer had any carpal tunnel pain at all. I was completely healed.

Thirty-five years later, I still am healed of wrist pain. I knit every day for hours and it never bothers me. I believe that anyone with the correct intention could also do this.

Your guides and angels are watching over you. Pay attention to their signs. Follow the trail of breadcrumbs and trust that it is all for the good. Even the painful and unpleasant parts of life might lead you to important turning points.

Barbara Ross Greaney

DANCING IN THE DARK WITH CROWS

*Y*ears ago, during the magical dusk hours, a burgeoning cluster of the large, black birds would fly through a valley adjacent to our nature sanctuary and beckon us with their caws. Whenever they did, my husband and I would wave to them, watching their pearlescent upper black wings glow in the setting sun's rays. Eventually, some of them would settle in our fir trees for a short visit before they took off to rejoin the rest of the flock. This bond, a timeless one, stays with me even now.

In my practice as an intuitive environmental consultant, I carefully watch for the signals and signs of nature on a site before I meet with a client. The clues and insights I receive from nature give me information that helps me in my work. In some cases, those messages have changed me forever.

On this day, it was my timeless friends, the crows, who arrived with news.

My client had requested a session to help her uncover the problem at her long-term, residential investment property. Although the setting looked outwardly serene, the tenants in these low-income bungalows had begun to bicker and many had moved away. Those who took their places had the same problems. She was perplexed at the troubled atmosphere taking over this seemingly peaceful setting.

I arrived early to give me time with nature, parking at the entrance so I could get a broad view of the entire, humming complex while providing space for nature's inhabitants to express any subtle clues about the character or quality of the ambiance. I opened my heart to a sensory, intuitive experience and took in the atmosphere. I felt a fertile quiet descend, sending a calm wave around the usually busy parking lot.

Immediately, large, somber crows—my familiar nature associates—started arriving and landing delicately on the complex electrical and telephone wires above the lot. Landing softly, four or five at a time, they fluttered a bit as each grouping secured their place, gradually creating a circle around me. They seemed united in an invisible bond, finding a common purpose on the wires. Once a tiny group had settled, more incoming bird messengers landed further down the wires, announcing their arrival in a gentle, whirling wind as they perched. When there were forty or so birds gathered, an enigmatic power circle became apparent. They remained mostly silent. Their energy was palpable, suggesting an upcoming strong warning that might be quite uncomfortable.

Crows are intelligent enough to understand complex human issues. On this day, their strong presence seemed to send the message, "The trouble here is hidden and not apparent to the owner." I listened deeply, letting them speak.

"Look for slight, unusual feelings and encounters as you walk. We will help you. A group of us came to support a change, as this trouble is bigger than it first appears. Resolving this trouble could be a great service to the area and to us. Be gentle, as the owner will not want to hear about this trouble."

I felt a surge of gratitude toward these creatures, who had somehow known I needed their help. I heard a message from them addressing this very thing.

"Thank you for asking for our help," they said. "Our past connection in the forest with you helped us respond."

Just as the message from the crows came through, right on time, my client came out for our meeting. As we started the tour, the crows silently maintained their presence with us. One by one, they flew farther out, expanding the strong field of quiet support surrounding the complex.

The owner began sharing her concerns. Everything on the surface looked fine, but I stayed curious and silently asked for further information through subtle signals.

Symbolically, crows can be an omen of change. They have firsthand knowledge of the higher order of the law. Sometimes crows arrive to support a more profound truth coming to the surface.

I felt prompted to search for minor inconsistencies in the surroundings. An uncomfortable feeling crept in as I spotted three cars parked irregularly in one corner of the lot. Just at that moment, a renter approached us with a cheery smile, ready to chat.

The property owner introduced him as one of the longtime residents. After we had exchanged greetings, I quietly asked him if he knew who owned the irregularly parked cars. He took me aside and said he felt the cars were part of an illegal drug transaction.

"Unknown cars usually arrive at dusk to exchange packages."

"Are people who live in the complex involved?" I asked.

"I don't want to stir up any trouble with neighbors. That why I've kept quiet."

I caught up to my hostess and shared the information. A glaze of anguish, disbelief, and shock washed over her. "I wanted to bring real renewal to this property," she sighed. "How could this be happening?"

Then I told her about the crows, who still stood silent guard in the nearby trees. She understood. Knowing about them seemed to unlock something in her, allowing her to let go of comfort and take on the courage to investigate this challenge in a broader sense.

That is what she did. She let local law enforcement know that her property was a new staging location for drug gangs. Their subsequent investigation illuminated a surprisingly large, city-wide problem, eventually leading to a resolution.

A new level of peace and clarity rose in her complex and in the entire city. And it had all begun when I acknowledged the wisdom from a benevolent circle of crows who alerted us to uncover a darker, uncomfortable level of truth.

Ann Marie Holmes

SEA BISCUIT

"They are the most ancient medicine," my Indigenous teacher and dear friend had once remarked about my lifelong passion for rocks.

The discovery of a particular stone has been an auspicious sign for me since childhood. Walking along the windswept beaches of the northwest, my father and I held hands and looked for the most precious of stones, the ones that seemed to harden light: agates. The presence of those rocks felt like Divinity. Each stone provided a thrill of joy and awe.

The rock beings once even guided me from the realm of the dream world. I dreamt it was twilight on the shoreline of a vast, calm sea. I saw a wispy, almost transparent young woman strolling along the tide line, reminiscent of my long, contemplative beach walks with my father and, later, my favorite homeland beach. At the woman's feet were round stones. As I looked more closely at them, I saw that each stone was a planet. The tremendous, calm sea beyond was a cosmos filled with stars.

After my first husband died, I first found solace on the long beach near our home in the woods. As I walked with my head down, tearful, sometimes morose, I prayed for a sign. I whispered aloud, "Answer me! Let me know I am not alone in this."

My heart called out in anguish for consolation. I yearned for the assurance of a relationship with the sacred, of belonging. I longed to be welcomed and to feel those mysteries and awe-inspiring communications with the unseen and natural world I felt as a child.

My sense of intimacy with a loving Divinity had been severely shaken after my husband's descent into addiction and death at thirty-five. My feeling of the Earth as my home became tainted.

I asked for an agate. Unknowingly I was asking for the transmutation of my grief into something beautiful, like the clear stone. In the tideline lay moss green, rosy, gray, striped, speckled, and brown rocks. A glimmering smooth agate would sometimes arise among them, and my anguish would be lifted, at least for a while.

Years later, I asked for another sign. My grown daughters had recently moved back to the wilds where they grew up. They each found a spot on the land to tuck in a trailer home. Their coming home felt right, signaling that healing in our family was in process.

Soon after they settled in, when meditating, the great mystery gave me a sign in the form of an inner image of a giant, glowing, golden stone with winding veins of white and traces of pure transparency within it. The stone waited deep in the warm earth, not yet ready to be above ground. At the surface of the land above the rock, I saw the ripples of small earthquakes. I took this vision as a sign of what would come: some shake-ups and some excavating of old family things, with stunning light and love at the core.

Seated around our cabin campfire, I shared this vision with my younger daughter. Two days after, I was back at the beach. I searched the stones with my eyes, and when I looked up, I saw a seal had been escorting me for several miles. I gazed down at the rocks, feeling their endurance and wisdom, and there was the palm-sized, oval golden, milky-and-clear stone. Here and there, streaks of its oval body were transparent. I knew that it was a sign and a symbol of family healing.

The rock was a miniature version of the stone in my inner vision. Heart warmed, I thanked the great mystery, and later that day, I gifted it to my youngest daughter.

The rock beings are allies. Three years ago, I traveled to the coast on the other side of the country, where my eldest daughter was practicing as a visiting nurse. She and her then-husband lived in a condominium temporarily as their relationship of many years continued its sad unraveling. The long, sandy beach in front of the multistoried building was a tourist haven that did not please my untamed soul, but it offered magnificent treasures. The beach was rife with fossils. In those stones, the life of long-ago, fragile living things had become eternal.

On the afternoon of my arrival, my daughter showed me her small trove of fossils sitting on the end of the granite kitchen counter. We shared the thrill of these material yet spirit-filled objects. Her prized discovery was a fossilized sea biscuit millions of years old. It resembled a familiar sand dollar, with the same flower design on top, but domed like a biscuit. She informed me she had researched sea biscuit fossils online and had discovered they are exceedingly rare.

The next day, I strolled the beach, welcoming the sea air and chilly winter sunlight. But I walked distracted by concern for my daughter and her spouse. Both good people, they were embroiled in painful patterns each seemed helpless to alter. I tried to turn my worry into prayer. I prayed for a sign for my daughter, a sign of hope unattached to my wishes or fears.

Feeling tired after a stroll of several miles, I ambled back toward the condominium building. When I paused to rest, I looked down at the pale sand. The edge of what appeared to be a curved shell peeked out. Leaning down, I brushed the sand away and scooped it up. It was an extraordinary gift, a rock blessing, an auspicious sign for me and my beloved, grown child.

It was a stone sea biscuit.

Dr. Joanne Halverson

HEALING REGRET

They say you never forget your first love, and it's true, at least for me. I met my love when I moved to Vancouver, Canada to attend a university. A friend introduced us, and that was all it took. We spent the next three years working, studying, and traveling together—with arguments and plenty of tears, too.

We backpacked through China during one school holiday break, a trip that would change the course of my life. We had a full-blown argument under the Eiffel tower. We began to say and do things that hurt and upset us both. At the end of three years, our love affair was over. I wanted to travel and live in Asia; he planned on settling in Vancouver.

I moved abroad and moved on. I fell in love again and so did he. We both eventually got married. I lost touch with him, but once a month, for years on end, his face would turn up in my dreams. I'd always awaken with an odd mix of emotions. I reached a point where I was tired of the dreams, especially when I had fallen in love again and was happy and content with my life in a new country. Why wouldn't he just stay in the past?

I enlisted help. I did cord-cutting and other ceremonies and used crystals and everything clever I could think of to get him out of my energy. Just when it would seem to work, I'd have another dream. I'd been told that when someone keeps popping up into your energy field, they are holding onto you. If that was the case, he seemed to be hooked in deep.

Eighteen years passed, eighteen years of dreams that faded only a little. I booked flights back to my birth country and got in touch with an old school friend, the mutual friend who had introduced me to him. Reconnecting with this friend triggered something, because before I knew it, the dreams were back, stronger than ever.

In the first dream, he and I met and were so happy to see each other. We spent the dream catching up on our lives, and I woke up with a smile, satisfied with this beautiful dreamtime reunion. But the following nights were less pleasant. In those dreams, I was trying to talk to him, and he was avoiding me. I woke up feeling terrible.

I considered reaching out in real life, but my instincts said that was a bad idea. I decided that the dreams where he refused to speak with me were a sign. *He doesn't really want to see me,* I thought. *But then why do I keep dreaming of him?* I knew the universe was trying to tell me something.

One day when I was driving to pick up my son from school, *Always on My Mind*, a Pet Shop Boys song came on the radio. It was a cover version of an old tune my stepfather used to play. I knew all the lyrics, and some of them instantly resonated. A week later, the same song came on the radio again as I was driving my son home. *This is no coincidence. The spirit world is really trying to get my attention.*

It wasn't uncommon for me to get song lyrics stuck in my head on a repeat loop. Sometimes a line or two would sing in the background of my brain for weeks on end, nearly driving me crazy. It was only after I had my spiritual awakening that I learned why this happened. When a song is stuck in your head, it's because there is a message for you there from the spirit world. Once I would figure out the message—poof!—the song would vanish without a trace, and soon, I couldn't even remember what the song had been.

Over the years, I'd gotten better at deciphering these song lyric messages. It was tougher with this Pet Shop Boys song, which lodged in my head for the next three weeks.

Eventually, I realized the song and the dreams were connected. I looked up the lyrics and read them as a story. A few lines jumped out at me. The song was about regret and how the songwriter hadn't tried hard enough to make his partner happy.

Did my first love remember our time together with deep regret? Was that why he couldn't stay out of my dreams, even after all these years? He was happily married with kids now. I realized that I might not have the story quite right.

I was on the edge of headache from the song, which at this point was practically shouting in my head. I sat in meditation, and I called in his higher self, and tried to connect with him on a higher level. I needed answers and clarity. I needed the song out of my brain, and him out of my dreams.

Why are you coming into my dreams? I asked him.

The song shouted on, during our telepathic communication, about giving me another chance.

When his higher self replied, it sounded so much like he did, but wiser. *I'm not choosing to come in. You keep calling me in, because you have things you haven't fully resolved.*

His message took me by surprise.

I have things to resolve? I thought you did! I telepathically replied.

All that happened between us, all those years ago—we have forgiven each other, I have forgiven myself, but you have not forgiven yourself, he said.

Oh!

The song played on, but more softly.

I realized now that he had never been the problem. It was me. I had regrets, and I had forgotten to forgive myself. I decided to send out the intention to the universe to help me find the most perfect time and place to show this act of compassion to myself.

Poof! went the song.

Poof! went the dreams.

A month later, I was back in my birth country. As I sat on a wooden dock overlooking a huge lake, I suddenly knew that I was ready. This was the time and place. I connected into the lake, the surrounding trees, the animals, and the mountains. I called in their support. A slight, cool breeze tickled my face as I did so. I went inward and found I could finally access those buried feelings of guilt, shame, and regret. I hadn't known I was carrying so much of this pain until I felt it surface in my consciousness.

Then I released these feelings to the breeze and the water, allowing space to bring in the self-forgiveness my soul was calling for. All around me, tiny fish began leaping, sending the surface of the clear water rippling out in all directions.

Fish show up as spirit animals when compassion, nurturing, and care are needed. They help us dig into things buried below the surface of our lives, so we can reconnect to them. I walked away from my fish guides with a peaceful feeling, knowing I was free to move forward in life.

I thought briefly of the Pet Shop Boys song, and now it sounded like a sweet memory from the past. I know the song, and the dreams of my first love, will not return, and I feel grateful that we are both healed.

Yolanda Tong

ECHOES OF TIME

When a burgundy jeep appeared in front of me again, I knew it was a sign. Seven more years had passed. But would my life blow up again?

Once again, I was packing boxes, between homes with no idea where I might land. A gypsy is always at home in a car, so I planned a road trip. As I pulled out of the driveway, saying goodbye to the last place I lived, I thought about traveling for a while. Newport had always called to my soul, so I headed north. I knew deep conversations with the universe were waiting for me.

The drive was full of positive signs, one confirmation after another. I arrived in Newport in the late evening, feeling aligned with where I was. Maybe this would be a fresh start for me. No matter how I had attempted to move forward in the prior few years, the past seemed to grip my ankles and pull me back.

The next morning, I walked through Newport with eyes of innocence, wondering what in my life was still incomplete. I sensed that a sign was on its way that would help me integrate the last cycle of my life and move to the next.

As I turned a corner, I saw a chilling sign. Across the street was a burgundy jeep. I knew this jeep. It seemed to turn up every seven years, and it foretold chaos and destruction. The original burgundy jeep represented the long term karmic relationship that stemmed back to when 11, 1111 and 111 began appearing. The second time it appeared was seven years later. Calculating in my head, I whispered, "Two echoes in time."

Black smoke billowed from beneath the vehicle's hood. I was speechless. *How is it possible that I am seeing this again? Didn't I already figure this out? Is another explosion about to happen here, and within my life? Is this a warning? Is it for healing? Is it the final integration? Had I reincarnated the exact same experience? Was everything that occurred seven years ago about to start all over again? Or was it about to reverse, and return everything that had been lost?* My mind was spinning.

I knew to relax, breathe, and feel as I sank into the memory of the last time the jeep had turned up. I chuckled softly as I considered the countless times clients had proclaimed, "I did this work already. I have done the work around letting them go. I am complete with that. I don't need to go there again." However, I know that I am never "done." A fragment of self must still be trapped in the old story.

We had arrived in Baltimore, Maryland; three women and two kids in an RV. My mission was to prove to myself and others that signs guide us if we let go and live organically. We called it "The Rebel Road: Connecting the Dots from What Was to What IS"— an eleven-month tour of sixty-six cities for my one-woman show. It was a completely off-the-cuff, in-the-moment, ad lib experience. Each performance was made up the universal conversations I encountered along the way.

It was the night before my first performance, which would be at a local college, followed by an appearance at a spiritual center. We were only ten miles from our first RV campsite stop, sitting at a red light, when a burgundy jeep sailed halfway through the large intersection and then stalled directly in front of me, approximately twenty-five feet away. Smoke started curling out from under the hood. The driver jumped out of the jeep and ran, as if he knew. Within the next minute, the jeep exploded right in front of us and its interior became engulfed in flames.

I was struck with a sudden awareness that this was a sign. Two weeks later, chaos erupted, obliterating many parts of my life. The intersection had represented a crossroads in my life. The old world would have to crumble completely, burning away to ash, before my new life could be born.

The explosion had been a sacred encounter; a guidepost that warned me of what was to come.

The next seven years were challenging, but everything that transpired was for my highest good. Life was calibrating me. My obstacles encouraged a level of independence I had not known before.

Now, another burgundy jeep had appeared with smoke billowing from under its hood. I intuited this experience was different. There was no fire, only smoke. I felt different within my body than I had before.

I knew life to be a blend of dark and light, and that darkness appears to restore balance and naturalness to life.

Residue from prior experiences had remained within my body, specifically in my gut; my engine. The universe was calling me to engage the inner work of releasing the remaining pain. I simply needed to feel into my gut, deepening into where it smoldered, and stay present until the energies dissolved.

I felt the residue absorb completely into the wholeness that I AM. My breath remained rhythmic. My body relaxed. I made it through, and knew that new life awaited me.

Just then, a song began playing from within a nearby cafe. The lyrics sang of loss and triumph—another perfect sign on this momentous day.

I walked away from the jeep, consciously walking toward a new unknown, knowing the past was behind me. "Alright universe," I whispered. "I am ready to shed the next layer of identity. Bring it on."

Simran

PART THREE

*Deepening Your Connection
with the Cosmos*

Train your eyes and ears; train your nose and tongue.
The senses are good friends when they are trained.

— BUDDHA

EXPANDING YOUR RELATIONSHIP WITH LIFE'S PROMPTS

How can you become more aware of signs and the messages they are bringing? Engaging with these life prompts may not feel natural in the beginning, but it can lead you to living in a more natural way. Your practice of conversing with the universe will undoubtedly return you to places of wonder, imagination, and playfulness. Although this kind of communication initially requires conscious presence, it will not be long before you realize these signs have existed as your nature all along.

The phenomena of signs occurs so that you more intimately engage co-creation and creativity. You are the journey. There is nowhere to go. Become present and rhythmic in your partnership with life. As time goes by, try not to look up the meanings for any signs that appear. Instead, close your eyes and notice what comes to you. Look at your life and contemplate how each sign applies.

Center within yourself. Bring presence to the universe within. Signs are constellations of your experience. Activate the cosmic grid between your inner and outer universe by seeing the mirrors that life is presenting. Dialogue from that grounded, centered position. You can always connect, in every way possible, and to everything that crosses your path. You do not have to go looking for signs—simply look for *you* in all that you see.

The following sections support opening to the signs that fill your world and describe contemplations, processes, and steps for deepening your relationship with signs. Relax into each experience. Enjoy the journey as each step expands your energy of receivership. Be patient and kind to yourself. Be loving and gentle. Even if you feel normal doubt and skepticism, try to maintain an expectant mindset.

CONSCIOUS FEELING

From the time you were a child, your feelings have been pushed down and repressed. Out of the need for self-protection, you learned to mask the self. This resulted in you ignoring and denying feelings when they rose. Sometimes, you might have partially felt things. Other times, you did not let yourself feel anything at all.

As we age through the stages of adolescence, young adulthood, and adulthood the little child remains stuffed down. Feelings sit within the cells. Emotions that are repressed remain and become the marinade flavoring each oncoming experience and encounter. The inner child still feels frightened, frozen, and in fear of punishment. However, it is the child within that possesses the ability to access and understand signs, synchronicity, and play. To fully awaken all of this, begin feeling, instead of denying, escaping, and suppressing.

The best way to begin feeling is to breathe. Your breath will bring greater presence to the body. You will notice where emotion and pain sit. In becoming aware, discern where your breath needs to be focused.

I find it is best to close my eyes when emotion rises. This way, the ego cannot use the eyes for distraction. Center within your body and simply feel the feelings. Locate where they are. If feelings and sensations begin moving to various parts of the body, follow them with your breath. This is a good practice for complex, dense emotions and for the lightest of them. It is also greatly supportive when dealing with anxiety, pain, or depression.

When you encounter a sign, or a trigger, allow for space and time to be with yourself. It is best to do this in the moment, before feelings and sensations fade into unconsciousness. Later, revisit the scenarios and review anything that held pain, remorse, regret, anger, or disillusionment. See what you have not been willing to see. Be with the images that were too strong to hold in the past.

Signs can bring you out of numbness. The universe desires you to feel, because without feeling; life stagnates. There can be no creation and little joy, creativity, and ease, because dense emotions weigh down higher frequency, lighter ones. Your sacred temple needs to be cleansed. Your goal is neutrality. To achieve this state, you must be cleared of emotional debris. Residual energies from trauma, pain and fear must be dissolved and absorbed back into the light of self.

Contemplate the following questions when encountering low-range, dense emotions that create discomfort, dis-ease, and pain. It can be beneficial to also ask these questions when experiencing high-frequency feelings of comfort, ease, and happiness. This enables you to break through all your conditioned ceilings.

1. What do I not want to face or feel?
2. What can I open to feeling more of?
3. Where is this feeling taking me?
4. What do I need to remember?
5. What truth has been forgotten?
6. Why is my soul bringing this up?
7. What is the next best, most loving step?

CONSCIOUS ASKING

Your presence of signs and symbols begins with asking. The ask might be unconscious. Unconscious asking comes through the energy being expressed, blocked areas of thought, and suppressed emotion. These disintegrated parts create signs that reflect obstacles and challenges you will be required to move through. They produce signs that bring awareness to non-integrated portions of self.

Asking also can be conscious and intentional. In these moments, you are calling yourself forward as much as you are calling forth signs from the universe. In consciously asking, focus your mind and heart upon open-heartedly holding inquiry. Then, patiently wait. Let life lead you forward.

Know your question. Ask the universe to reveal guidance. Hold a space of expectancy and gratitude for being heard. If you want specific proof, ask for that to be shown to you. Let go of any attachment. Remain open, conscious, curious, and aware. Trust, and have fun.

Signs can also reflect misalignment, indicating where you are not congruent in thought, feeling, and action. This is why conscious inner work and self-awareness are so important. Life is much gentler once you get to know yourself. Living in a constant state of default is tumultuous and will bear signs reflecting chaos. Experience integrates new ways of being, thinking, feeling, and behaving.

Affirmations are a great technique, but if your feelings and actions are not aligned, they are of little use and your manifestations will be haphazard. Outward positivity that carries an undercurrent of negativity might seem to create positive situations. However, the chance of self-sabotage and mishap increases because of the underlying negativity.

All signs present opportunities to heal, grow, and align. As you continue your areas of personal growth, higher expressions of manifestation will occur. As you gain greater mastery, you will be called to higher and higher degrees of alignment. As you overcome one level of challenge, you will be presented with more to transcend. It is dependent upon the mission of your soul in this lifetime. Whatever occurs, signs will appear for you.

Do not be fooled by the appearance of those who struggle. You have no idea what their level of awareness is, nor are you privy to their frequency or vibration. It is best to focus on yourself. Do not judge anyone's journey. You do not know their soul, their life intention, or what they must heal for their bloodlines.

Experience the journey of growing and changing into an empowered, compassionate witness. You are a process within a process. In the moment of asking, you are freeze-framing time so that a series of signs can begin appearing. Be present to what you intend and ask for. Then, be open to however that unfolds. You have no control. You never did. If something appears that you do not like, remember, you are being cleared of blocks that no longer serve you.

CONSCIOUS LISTENING

All answers, creation, and manifestation stem from your interior. Turn inward, and tune in. Notice how your thoughts and feelings reflect outwardly. Moments of quiet encourage self-realization. Signs are another aspect of self to be realized. This reframe prepares your mind for greater access to intuition.

A clear, conscious decision to pay attention and be present is your next step. This is a commitment. It is an act of continual self-love. It means being aware when signs present themselves. It requires listening on every level and from every dimension.

Immediately after receiving a sign, pay attention to everything that happens. What you experience will intersect with intuition and create understanding. Listen to what the sign says in the first moment. Listen for what you were thinking in the moment prior to the sign appearing. Finally, cultivate deep acceptance that everything—every thing—in your experience is offering a message in some way. Remain in the inquiry. Everything in your experience is language and you are in a continuous conversation.

Listening is both a physical and intuitive tool. Direct revelation is a higher kind of listening. This is another way of engaging your inner senses. When deep communion is present, higher listening can enter. When there is no separation between you and what is in front of you, a small voice will speak through the silence. Listening must be whole-bodied, encompassing sight, sound, sensation, and intuition.

Signs will appear so that you take notice and say, "Okay, this is interesting! Did that really just happen?" Your attention will be drawn to certain things. In a moment, you will look up, turn around, or bump into something. Your eyes will land on something. You will hear something in a very present way. The moment will bring about a sensation, pause, or a feeling of complete presence.

Remember, you are not to search out signs. They appear when needed. Your inner guidance will bring you to them. This is a process that requires relaxation and ease rather than tension and force. When something in your external environment catches your attention, you have accessed a kind of listening. Listening can be experienced through physical sensations as well, such as muscle tension, spontaneous body reactions, tastes, or smells. You may hear your inner voice or see images in your mind's eye. The items themselves may speak to you.

As you think about life from these different perspectives, your perception will expand. Listen deeply, attentively, and patiently. Observe what comes through the ordinary world that suddenly feels extraordinary. Begin attuning to the mystical energy of self, life, and the universe through the current of sound. Pay attention to the nuances of experience. Release expectations so you receive what is meant to come through. Let listening become an experience of moment-by-moment presence.

CONSCIOUS INTEGRATION

In every relationship, there is an exchange. You receive something and you give something. When the universal concept of giving-and-receiving is performed with gratitude and conscious awareness, an ordinary exchange is elevated to a higher level of reciprocity. The principle of reciprocity is especially important when working with signs. You are engaging in a sacred partnership. Each time you receive a sign from the universe, the universe receives more of you.

As you receive from the universe, contemplate your greater purpose. Give life the best of you. This means becoming the most aligned energy vortex that you can be. Although you seek to receive signs that guide your steps, do not forget that you are also a sign for others to do their work. Your actions might guide their steps or give them a chance to peer into the mirror that you present.

Your consciousness expands when you bring what is unknown into the space of being known. Your next step is conscious integration, which means consciously living. Walk your talk. Do your work. Choice is a great power. Choosing consciously brings forth superpowers.

Life is always supporting you. Spirit is always guiding you. Most importantly, your soul continually places breadcrumbs upon your path. Signs break past worldly illusions to answer many of your questions and allow for heart-based living. These consistent and constant connections increasingly enhance inner joy and fulfillment.

So don't take life so seriously; lighten up! The universe is playing with you. It is having a conversation in, as, and through you. You are part of a universal tapestry, a sacred story of all time. You are not alone, and never have been.

PRACTICES FOR DEEPENING YOUR EXPERIENCE WITH SIGNS

• —— • ◉ ◉ ◉ • —— •

*W*e live in a most exciting time. While a great deal feels unknown, possibility feels palpable. You are a master magician possessing the ability to wield innate Divine energy. Opening to this co-creative power with life leads to new pathways of self-empowerment. The following sections will assist you in recognizing yourself within each sacred encounter.

Now you have discovered signs really are presenting themselves, and that these sacred encounters are very real experiences you can tap into for guidance. But how can you make this a normal part of life? Although you may perceive the world of form as separate, everything surrounding you is the Divine in form—and you are, as well.

Earth is a sacred space in which to learn. You are not being *tested*; you are being *expanded*. Every experience is designed to touch you multidimensionally. This is how life leads you toward your highest expression. This "You-niverse City" of Earth is for you.

RELAXATION

Expect signs, but do not demand them to appear. Do not push or will signs to appear. Do not go hunting for them. Do not become overly analytical. Do not become too serious. Do not turn your life into a research project. The universe need not be coerced. It will just happen. Everything is a process, and you are the journey. This is a process of gentleness, ease, and play. It should be fun. A sense of humor is required.

Open your heart and experience the play and pleasure available to you. Play unfolds as you let go of control, seriousness, and disbelief. It is important to understand some ground rules. Just as there are ways to open yourself to signs, symbols, and synchronicity… there are also behaviors that close you off from them.

These behaviors come from an imbalance of masculine shadow energy, which blocks receptivity. Healthy, feminine nature is receptive. To expand the journey of self-awareness, the battle between your own inner masculine and feminine must be balanced. If operating from an imbalanced masculine state, your feminine energy will match that with an equivalent shadow state. Be aware of how your energy is expressing disbelief or doubt.

Complete mental and physical relaxation can only be experienced by going within and connecting with a higher power. Completely surrender. If you want an answer or sign from the universe on a specific topic, release your attachment to the answer. Just allow it to come. Allow the experience to be more important than the answer you gain.

EMBODIMENT

The physical vessel must be prepared. You might be unaware of how out-of-body you are. It is important to develop a practice of checking in with your physical presence. Several times a day, it may be necessary to bring your spirit back down into your body.

Throughout the day, we all leave our bodies, This occurs anytime we become frightened, stressed, anxious, or depressed. It also occurs when we are distracted or multi-tasking. Being imbalanced or living beyond your natural rhythms also causes us to disconnect. Continually checking a cellphone contributes to disembodiment.

With the continual distractions of life, such as technology, it is necessary to develop a practice for becoming present and spirit-embodied. The following exercise is a wonderful way to become more present, while also relieving stress.

AN EMBODIMENT PRACTICE

1. Begin by standing.
2. Remember to breathe throughout the exercise.
3. With the palms of your hand, firmly pat your entire body.
4. Begin with the head and move toward the feet, spending about fifteen to thirty seconds in each area.
5. Pat the crown of your head and move down the face to the jaw area.
6. Pat down the neck and onto the collarbone, shoulder area and behind the neck.
7. Move up and down each arm two to three times, making sure to tap both the underside and the outer arm.
8. Move to the torso, patting down the front of the chest, up and down both sides; and then moving to your back.
9. Once completing your back, pat your buttocks, hips, and lower belly.

10. Spend extra time in the belly area, as this is the center point of the Hara line and prime energy center for the soul. The area around your navel is the single most powerful place to focus and pool energy.

11. Breathe several times in and out of the navel area, while imagining your essence being pulled down and in.

12. Move to the thighs, tapping to the knee on all sides, including the back of the legs.

13. Tap around the knees, and proceed down the shins, calves, and sides of the lower leg.

14. Sit down and tap your ankles and feet, especially the bottoms of your feet.

15. Rub the soles vigorously and breathe deeply as you bring the soul all the way down.

16. Place both feet upon the ground and while sitting, stomp your feet on the ground as if you were running in place. Do this for thirty seconds to a minute.

17. When finished, close your eyes, and breathe. Feel the difference in your body.

18. Take notice of how much more present you are; and how much more grounded you feel.

DAY DREAMING

Day dreaming prepares your mind by creating a consciousness of expectancy and possibility.

1. Relax and close your eyes.

2. Anchor your attention within your heart.

3. Breathe from the Earth, inhaling through the feet and up into the heart.

4. Exhale from the heart up and out of your crown, toward the universe.

5. Inhale from the universe back into the crown, and back into the heart.

6. Exhale from the heart, releasing the breath through the soles of your feet.

7. Continue the breath in this manner, relaxing into an even, rhythmic connection between the inner and the outer.

8. Close your eyes and focus your attention on the third-eye point.

9. Begin daydreaming about nature and notice what appears.

10. Let the daydream take you where it desires; notice where it takes you and what it shows you.

11. Allow images within the daydream to become prominent, but do not hang onto them. Simply let them light up in some way, becoming enhanced, and then softening back into the dreamscape.

12. Do not judge or analyze, just feel.

13. Do not make anything happen; notice what occurs.

14. When you are complete with your visualization, make notes about what popped out in your day dream.

15. Try daydreaming different environments: the beach, the mountains, your home, a place of work, a shopping street.

16. Let your imagination lead. You are priming your subconscious to speak.

One of the easiest ways to notice signs is by cultivating where the subconscious already speaks to you, in your night dreams. So much symbolism appears within the sleep state. There are signs galore. Whether you dream vividly, only remember glimpses, or do not seem to dream at all... a dream journal will support you in learning the subtlety of imagery conversation. Upon waking, make a note of the signs and remnants of your dream, if any.

If you are someone who believes you never dream, or if you can hardly remember dreams, keep a journal that focuses on feeling rather than dream specifics. Journal about what you feel; or what you might have felt while sleeping. In doing this, you signal your subconscious to begin remembering. By getting more into your body, you open to dreaming.

Additionally, each night before falling asleep, do two things: Set an intention and tell your mind and body to dream. Second, anchor into a feeling of joy and expectancy as you drift off to sleep.

A DREAM JOURNAL

Upon awakening from the dream:

1. Remain relaxed with your eyes closed and breathe.
2. Anchor into the feelings that were activated through the dream.
3. Do not analyze anything yet.
4. Simply reflect upon the dream and how you feel.
5. Allow the images of greater significance to pop out at you.
6. Write down the details you remember in your dream journal.
7. Take three deep breaths and set an intention to interpret the dream that is supportive to your highest self and higher learning.
8. Journal for twenty minutes, if possible.
9. To satisfy an inquiring mind, look up symbolism in a dream book.
10. If awareness arises from your research, add that to your journal.

Dreams typically reflect an issue that you are dealing with. They arise to support resolution. Remember, everyone and everything in your dream is always... you.

RESEARCHING

It is natural to go to the extreme and begin seeking out answers for everything. Initially, you might become caught up in researching every little sign that appears. If you want to know what specific things mean, there are plenty of resources on and offline. It is alright to get this linear understanding. There are many resources that provide generalizations which fit all people. You can Google the spiritual meaning of almost anything, not to mention the host of books and card decks available. You can also inquire with intuitive sign readers. Take advantage of the resources that help bring meaning to things in the beginning.

Once you have gotten past the initial excitement of signs appearing and have gotten used to the general meanings through research, consider tapping into your own intuition. That beginner level of research and understanding satisfies the ego for a time. However, do not become overly dependent on outer resources or you fall into the trap of seeking. Instead, do the work to cultivate knowing. Deepen your understanding beyond the quick fix of looking things up. Integrative, heart-gut comprehension is what will change your world. Move past the constraints of intellectual understanding and logic.

Build a practice of inner inquiry before looking up the answer to each bird, tree, and number you come across. You may find it interesting how spot on you are when it comes to meanings and insight. Take a breath. Check in with yourself. Remember, you always have plenty of time to figure it all out. This is about connecting: to your intuition, to your world, to the greater universe living inside of you. You will gain an intuitive understanding of what things mean.

You will reach a point where you no longer need to look anything up. You will drop out of your head entirely and simply enjoy the experience of connecting so intimately with life.

CONNECTING THE DOTS

*ow that you're getting information from the universe, what can you do with it? How can you figure out what sign goes where and how to read it?

Do not look at these experiences as something to do. This book has been written to delight you into the mystery of your unique journey. Each story models this mystical process. Do not look at signs as another *task*. They are an invitation, courting you into greater oneness with the world. Life consists of a series of dots that expands the individual landscape so that it broadens our collective horizon.

While your signs and messages might seem like a string of separate occurrences, they connect. As signs increase in frequency, you will realize this universal language has its own set of nouns, verbs, adjectives, and endings. There will be times of long, drawn-out conversations that are filled with awareness, answers, and "aha's!" Other moments will leave you questioning. Some conversations might sound as if they are resonating from a loud, blaring megaphone, but most of them will land as soft whispers, a warm touch, and gentle grace that leave you feeling warm and fuzzy.

In noticing how signs relate to one another, you will begin connecting the dots. This expands your dialogue with life. As dots are connected, you will feel more integrated in, as, and to life. You'll also slip into greater discovery of how experiences within different areas of your life connect. As you see a shift in one sector of life, other sectors will also improve. In time, you will experience your conversation with the universe as a continuous interaction.

This is an opportunity to be present to what is around you, touching you all the time. Signs are in the energy and the air. They are textures, scents, and odors. They rest within plain sight and hide in both the visible and the invisible. Signs are sounds: soft, noisy, harmonious, and ecstatic. They are filled with flavor: savory, sweet, tart, and bitter. You will become acquainted, bit by bit. Then, you will desire more.

YOUR TREASURE MAP

Before incarnating, your soul put forth an intention: "I will not get lost. I will see signs along the way. These signs will be sacred encounters that lead me back to center. They will occur as Divine guideposts, turning points, and pathways. I am open to all experience, including opportunities where I might fragment, for the purpose of a more varied experience.

"I long to know the full spectrum of all that is, from the highest light to the densest of darkness. I long to be experience, perspective, and perception. I want to know judgment and neutrality. I desire to experience all that is beautiful within every expression that Essence can create. I long to know individuality and oneness. I desire a full integration of the senses, humanity, and remembering of Divinity.

"Within that infinite dialogue, signs, symbols, and synchronicities will exhibit a cosmic grid of awareness. Along the way, as pieces and parts come home, I shall place the puzzle pieces back together, and reclaim wholeness."

With that said… you became: the tree that falls, the butterfly that flies, and the dog that barks. You are the knee pain, the cough, and blurred vision. You are the leaky faucet, the rotting floorboard, and the clogged plumbing. You are the flat tire, the fender bender, and the empty gas tank. You are the angry store clerk, the admired celebrity, and the innocent babe. You are the clouds, the rainbow, and the eagle that soars. You are the rose, the majestic mountain, and an ocean of insight. You possess the ability to change with the seasons and become seasons of change. You are the elements, the weather, and each moon cycle. Each of these is a sign, and yet each is also a mirror of you. These mirrors, these aspects of self, are revealing you, to you.

The truth is, you are creation, creating itself. You were created in the image and likeness of the Creator. You have the Creator's DNA. You are in essence—Essence! You are that! You possess the same creative capacity as the universe from which you are born. This is your inheritance. Creation anointed you to inherently touch and express this Divine lineage. Glean more of who you are from every experience.

Connecting signs and symbols to your mythological story is an ever-deepening process, which expands with your availability to receive. You are not only increasingly supported by life, but also given signs that connect with one another to form an ongoing conversation of much larger proportion. Stringing together your breadcrumbs will produce volumes within your life story.

Create a diary of the signs that you can recall. Get to know yourself better. Get to know your signs. This exercise will build your intuition. It will also support you in seeing connections. After completing this exercise, you can begin connecting the dots of your own sacred mythology.

Signs are not random moments unattached to anything else. They weave and waft, revealing the rich, colorful, and textured journey of you. Putting your language of signs together creates a treasure map of experience where the true *you* is the hidden gold. Signs weave a thread within the story of your life. They become part of your mythology. Signs will connect as dots to create an interconnected dialogue between your inner and the outer worlds.

As you begin experiencing your conversations with the Universe, maintain a scrapbook or diary of what appears. I snap pictures of signs I encounter. It keeps the joy and magic of moments lingering long after they have occurred. It also helps me to see how signs connect with one another over time.

Signs are not exclusive. They build upon one another to create their own story. Sometimes the guidance that you are seeking will come through a string of signs. You may document signs through pictures, sketches, notes, or feelings. A scrapbook or visual diary can support returning to specific moments and feelings of discovery.

A JOURNAL OF SACRED ENCOUNTERS

1. Keep a journal, jotting down what randomly catches hold of your eyes, ears, or hands.
2. List things that bring "aha!" moments. This might be a word or inspiration that makes you feel something.
3. Note things that cross your path or give you pause.
4. When you have an issue or want assistance, ask a question out loud, with intention. Then write it down in your journal, expecting an answer. Take note of what happens and how that connects to your question.
5. Be cognizant of the songs, books, cards, billboards, or things that your eyes naturally land on when contemplating something.
6. Notice what comes your way. Notice how you feel at that moment. Connect to where it is in your body. Ask yourself what this sign—item, person, or experience—is trying to show you, about you.

7. What are you being called to embody and incorporate into your life?

STAYING IN THE INQUIRY

My intention is for you to develop your connection to signs in an even greater way. Develop your intuition. Practice by taking the first thought that comes to mind as your answer. That is always your soul speaking to you. Then feel. Your greatest guidance system is your feeling nature. Staying in the inquiry is a beautiful way to build your intuition and understanding.

The Crucial Questions

1. Where am I in "that?"
2. What is "that" showing me, about me?
3. What is it calling forth from within me?
4. What gifts, skills, or talents is that mirroring to me?
5. What is the universe saying to me?

Numbers

1. What numbers do you repeatedly see?
2. Journal what these numbers mean to you.
3. Make a list of prior addresses, so that you see what those numbers were showing you, about you.
4. What number has consistently been appearing lately?

The Human Body

1. What health issues have you faced in the past? How did that relate to what was occurring in your life?
2. Which side of your body has been most affected? (The left side is feminine; the right side is masculine.)

3. What current health issues surround you? What do all of these tell you about you?

4. What are the health issues of your pet, your children, or your immediate family saying to you, about you?

5. What feeling arises when you focus on individual ailments?

Art

1. Look at the art within your home. How did these foretell of experiences which manifested?

2. What images are within your workplace? How have these materialized for you?

3. Notice what you have been given as gifts or have given as gifts.

4. Notice what you feel when looking at different items within your home.

Songs

1. What songs you are drawn to?

2. What messages do the most recent songs give you?

3. What are they asking you to feel?

4. Where is that in your body?

Books

1. What books are coming to you?

2. What do their titles say to you?

3. Has a sequence of books come forward as a guiding message?

Movies

1. What movies or shows are you watching?

2. What do their titles say to you?

3. What feelings are arising?

4. Has a sequence of themes come forward as a guiding message?

Your Life Story

1. Identify your *pebble, rock,* and *boulder* moments.
2. What were these moments attempting to show you? How were they guideposts, turning points, or pathways?
3. What patterns and behaviors had to shift during these sacred encounters?
4. What cycles and rhythms have you become aware of within your life?
5. Take time to write your life story.

Deepening into greater intimacy and subtlety offers a rich conversation of powerful meaning. A unique dialect exists between you and the universe. Through this, standard meanings take on a deeper nuance intended for your understanding. Signs will support you in interacting with the world in a whole new way.

A SIGN OF THE TIMES

ow, more than ever before, the world is hurtling toward a time of remembrance. It is a bit of a bumpy ride, which is why you must utilize life and all its signs as a gauge for where you are. Life is your built-in barometer for measuring where you are mentally, emotionally, spiritually, and energetically. Simply watch what is appearing. Do not engage your judging mind when challenging circumstances manifest.

Earth is designed to continually grow and stretch you. With increasing self-awareness, you become more sensitive. This makes the world seem more intense. It is not. Illusion, deception, and injustice seem to have increased. They have not. You are becoming more conscious. With each step in my journey, I became more conscious, sensitive, and intuitive. This will happen for you as well. As it does, you'll awaken to higher levels of creative capacity, intuitive mastery, and correspondence with the universe.

We live in a world that tells us to live fast, do more, and remain positioned in overdrive. It often goes unnoticed that this fast-paced, multitasking behavior and continual doing stems from shadows we hold within. True enjoyment and fulfillment of life come from pauses, slowing down, and being present. It is necessary to temper the balance between shadow living and being present.

Take your time with things. Take walks. Be passionate. Do not panic. Take walks. Slow your reactivity. Take walks. Respond to life by being awake and aware. Did I mention taking walks? Take as many a day as you can. It will support the return of your natural rhythm. Your only job is to live well. This means honoring yourself. It also means honoring life, others, and the essence within all things. Let life in. Receive the signs that are around you.

Signs arise to support you in slowing down. They help you become more present. Do not default to your old habits and behaviors of drive and conditioned response. Be diligent. Be devoted. Be disciplined. Every experience in life is leading in the direction of your highest self. Regardless of what appears, signs will be present to lead, guide, and protect you. When you make the choice to trust life, you are also choosing to trust the experiences of your life. This also means trusting that signs will come, and that you will understand their guidance. You are not alone.

Signs align with your intuitive nature. They support spiritual growth and development. Partnership with the world is part of that growth cycle. You do not just come from life—you *are* life. Remember, your inherent connection is your aliveness within spirit. There is nothing more powerful than aligning with the creative force which animates you.

Our world appears topsy-turvy. We have felt stress, frustration, or exhaustion from what the world has illustrated in recent years. Change is constant. The discomfort and frenzy that is often palpable is a sign of our times. It is pointing in one distinct direction. These "signs" specifically point to moving inward. Yes, even the chaotic mirrors are signs. Each one of us is being called to move more deeply into the heart.

You have two distinct calls to action that are tied to one another. You are to listen for your dreams and desires. But you must truly slow down, listen, look, feel, and receive what is within.

The truth is that no single moment is unrelated to anything else. Nothing is random. Your life appears to occur in vignettes of experiences and individual capsules of story. Yet these are all built upon one another. These incidents are not separate, and neither are others in your experience. From the moment you are born, piece by piece, the entirety of you is being created.

Every moment of my life has been building who I am today. Simran is composed of every experience and each sign in between. The same is true for you. Every job, relationship, and experience create a significant memory in your cellular structure. Who you are today would be different without any one of those moments. Experiences over time—those of both tragedy and triumph—climax to unfold an experience that is larger than you.

Everything you encounter has a multidimensional component. This exists within each experience, sign, and insight. You could choose any moment, or a specific sign, to be the focus of a lifetime's contemplation. But humans are not wired that way. Our attention spans are short. Distraction is everywhere. We all love a good story and yearn to experience the hero's journey. To be truthful, people also love drama, intrigue, and romance. This is part of the human condition, and yet it also holds the makings of the mysticism, magic, and sacredness

I chose a string of stories to include in this book that illustrate an individual mythology. These experiences portray how signs build upon one another. They offer a holistic and global look into themes, extended across decades, that bring insight at the correct time. Every moment, each sign, and all experience are Divine orchestrations for a sacred story.

The last decade has held many mystical occurrences and serendipitous insights. Each moment has built the capacity for us to receive sacred "aha!" moments, Divine giggles, and mystical awe.

I converse with the universe and I also step back and engage expectancy without attachment. We must settle into how confirmations and overarching insights come through the most mundane, material objects. The idiom "One man's trash is another man's treasure," is quite true, as you will see.

Remaining in Newport a while longer, I walked everywhere and enjoyed the sights, sounds and smells of the area. With many signs and symbols appearing, the universe and I continued playing with one another. Play was exactly what I needed, as I was nearing the end of an expansive cycle of personal and spiritual growth. I contemplated how events and signs throughout my entire life linked together as my mythology; each piece filling a vast and intricate puzzle. As I did, weeds of fear and doubt began to sprout.

The period between 2012 - 2021 brought forth a deluge of signs, and great opportunities for spiritual mastery and growth. A series of events catalyzed tremendous change, bringing about another profound calling. Between 2013— 2020, I embodied an immersive and solitary exploration of the void. I had no agenda, no plan, and never dreamed I would write again. After completing this journey of dissolution and remembrance, I was guided to write. At first questioning this because I had no desire, I ultimately surrendered to the guideposts that continued appearing.

Upon committing, I told the universe that I would write, but I would not search for a publisher. After what had occurred, I simply did not have it in me to return to the "control-oriented, push forward" way of the world. Since inner guidance had brought forth "tables of content" for a trilogy, three books would be created. My next request to the universe was that all three books find one publishing home and that they all publish within an eighteen-month time frame.

I began writing without attachment to ever being published. As directed, I wrote a multidimensional dissection of soul instruction for navigating the conditioned human's return to humanity for accessing true enlightened expression. I did not think beyond the creative process. I did not look ahead or get caught up in who, what, where, when, or how this would manifest. I remained focused on the work until it was complete.

A publisher arrived purely through my asking and being patient. They contacted me unexpectedly. The same had occurred with other books I had written. Upon hearing of my project, they wanted all three books, and they said the books would be released within a fourteen-month span, since it was a trilogy. This synchronous flow was further confirmation that I had correctly followed guidance.

However, now that the trilogy was with the publisher awaiting production, I questioned them. The information I shared was radical and bold. I began wondering if writing them was part of my integration process, the ego's hidden agenda, or truly my higher service to humanity. I paused, sitting on a bench in the park. I prayed for confirmation, one way or the other. When complete, I continued exploring the area.

Although the day was warm and bright, there were not many people milling about. I felt a strong nudge to turn down the next side street. After several blocks, a sign appeared. It gave me pause. A huge rocking chair sat on the lawn. It was approximately thirty feet high and was bright lime green.

I immediately intuited that the color symbolized the high heart and personal power. I closed my eyes and breathed in the rocking chair to intuit the words "wise elder, childlike, and playful."

A man and a woman stood beneath the massive chair, taking photographs. Each wore a knapsack. They appeared miniature next to this grand art piece. The woman began climbing up the chair leg so she could sit in the grand, open seat. The gentleman remained below, tinkering with his camera. Soon after, he pointed it upward to photograph the woman. I chuckled, *This is who we are; BIG BEINGS pretending to be tiny creatures, who are always reaching for something higher as a distraction rather than self-recognition.* I smiled, knowing the universe was playing with me.

I closed my eyes, taking three deep and soulful breaths, and placed the man and woman in my heart, so that I might receive guidance for what they represented. I centered my inner vision on the camera which hung against the man's heart. The message quickly came: *Life is perceived and captured in snapshots. What is seen through the small human lens is held onto and carried as memory inside. This memory places weight upon the heart, bringing heaviness to subsequent similar images of life. Life's cycles and echoes are this over-exposure duplicated repeatedly.*

I moved my presence to the knapsacks, as that was the second item I'd noticed when walking up. *Heavy baggage causes aches, pains, and illness. This is the emotional debris, dust, and mental confusion that we carry, collecting more while journeying through life. Life holds challenges, obstacles, heartbreak, and things that seems to occur for no reason. But the initial energy causes the ripple. If you carry moments beyond their time, no one else is hurting you. You are hurting yourself, and on many levels. Don't carry this weight. Let each moment be what it is, and let it go. Everything is experience, just experience. Let it come; let it go.*

I continued to breathe deeply, asking about the man and the woman. *Masculine and feminine are present within each person. They are never out of balance. When holding the smallness of both energies, you are codependent, wounded, and shadowed. When holding the higher expression, you are interdependent, balanced, and healthy. Masculine and feminine always meet as equals. They express equally as shadow or as light. Life can only operate in the equilibration of checks and balances.*

This was one of the themes shared within my trilogy. But I was still questioning. Was this sign about the books, or pointing toward further unification of my masculine and feminine aspects? I needed clarity. I spoke out loud, as this usually achieved quickened responses.

"I hear you," I said. "Clearly show me if this is confirmation of the books, or for my personal path. Show me in a way that I cannot deny the clarity of your message."

I held a feeling of joy, gratitude, and expectation in my heart for several minutes, feeling my heart and energy expand as large as all of Newport.

I continued walking, knowing that I would receive a response, completely unattached to when it would arrive. Later that day, I met up with a new acquaintance. We were invited to a lovely home belonging to a sea captain. Upon arrival, I saw that he was transforming all that was old into something new. Another reflection.

THE CALLING

The mystery is the soil where genius grows. Discover your sacred spark. Resistance to life creates separation from your true and natural self. In fully living the life you are given, you begin to understand. This is the golden key.

Life is a barometer for measuring degrees of mastery. This does not mean mastering your ability to climb ladders of achievement, keep up with the Joneses, or ascend to the top of hierarchical structures. Life is not concerned with attaining medals, acquiring degrees, or receiving accolades. Earth is created as an experience for your soul, not your ego. Material accomplishments might become part of your experience. but are not your primary purpose.

Do not be bamboozled by shiny objects, golden handcuffs, or spangly baubles of superficiality. These glittering objects have created amnesia. The world is exactly as it was designed to be. "Stuff" will occur externally, because that is the way of the Earth plane. The world is designed to rock your boat. This built-in barometer measures where you are mentally, emotionally, spiritually, and energetically. Simply watch what is appearing. Utilize life and all its signs as a gauge for where you are. Do not engage the judging mind when challenging circumstances appear. People are not asleep. They simply have not awakened to themselves yet.

Mastery is an ascending staircase. The higher you go, the greater your access to the subtle and invisible. You will continue encountering experiences that invite greater mastery. Within these moments, depend on your conversations with the universe. Sometimes, the signs will seem bizarre, in other moments, unbelievably beautiful or funny. Take everything in stride. Surf the waves as the master you are.

Extensive renovations were underway at the sea captain's home. This felt like a wink and a nod from the universe. My old life had been transforming into something new. I winked and nodded back.

I was immediately struck by a huge pile of junk that had been strategically compiled in the front yard. Items he no longer wanted had been layered into a large, wooden structure. A bonfire was planned for the night's full moon. To me, this was "sign"'-age. The universe had delivered a response, and with quite a sense of humor! The conversation was full on! I could only imagine the laughter spreading throughout the cosmos.

Atop the heap was another chair. It was a very small, child-sized little rocking chair. It was paint-chipped and very worn. To the right of the heap was a third chair which sat on the lawn. This one was a slightly worn, white Adirondack chair. It appeared as if sitting laid back, witnessing and waiting. It was not part of the artful heap; but was close enough to watch the fire and feel the heat.

This seat represented the seeker who exists between the small chair and the BIG chair. It symbolized the identity who is focused in the world. This human part of us lives externally and carries goals and ambitions… stories, insecurities, and inequities… and our dreams, visions, and desires. It also represents our unconscious ways of living. The full moon occurring that evening also represents our unconscious mind. The bonfire was illustrating how we must willingly burn off the junk, old baggage and smallness that has been carried.

The smallest chair represented the tiny, self-absorbed, wounded child that is rocked by its constricting and painful stories. This "little rocker" has literally rocked the boat! When allowing all illusions to be recognized and dissolved into ash, the phoenix rises, humanity flowers and the Divine eagle spirit ascends to the top of the mount.

There is a reason the BIG chair is not in the same place as these two. Neither of these seats of consciousness could exist in the grandness of the Mighty Self. Each would have to be completely annihilated to embody the presence, immensity and truth of the Higher Self.

It takes courage to let go of the small insignificant self, and the middle mediocre Self to rise to such heights. BIGness requires posturing in the seat of consciousness where Divine nature reigns with the humble power of presence.

The Universe had spoken loud and clear in its response to my inquiry.

Amidst the dense, material, and dual world, the impossible becomes possible. Delight in all of it. Whatever appears in front of you is a sign of the times. You will begin to see the miraculous. Signs appear that will seem unbelievable. Let these moments expand your heart. Let each miraculous moment court the Divine within you.

Mastery manifests as grounded fortitude amidst emotional waves. It is the joyful core of satisfaction that subdues the mind's psychosis and reactivity. Victory is steady patience, a calm essence, and a compassionate constitution. It is love in action—holy love, tender love, intimate love, soft love, empathic love, and fierce love—in the wake of everything that exhibits non-love.

BEYOND GOOD AND EVIL

Is there good and evil in the world, or are these things merely reflections of energy? We each suppress emotions and energies that are then forced to come out through others. As a species, we must end the divisiveness and find the place where the dual nature of reality is recognized within oneness. Wholeness consists of yin and yang, dark and light, good and evil, and everything in between.

When moving beyond identities and stories—soaring high above all things—an incredible mosaic can be seen. Each person is an intricate piece in a grand and beautiful saga. There is no duality, light, dark, good, bad, or evil. What appears through many individual parts is one image that is textured and layered, beautiful and mesmerizing. It is an extraordinary cosmos of consultations, a universal art-scape with an array of intricate human strokes that create an architectural, sculptural, moving installation.

Life has an intricate and subtle way of getting our attention. Those you encounter are having to play a part in the cleansing of energies. If we were each to do the inner work in recognizing all parts of being, then others would be freed from having to play the roles of victim, villain, and sinner. Is there evil in the world? We can believe that and continue to point fingers, creating more of the same. We could also stop projecting that onto our world.

When we recognize evil, it is because something unknown is taking up residence. When seeing negativity, it is because negativity is held inside and wielded in some manner upon the self or other. When we see love, kindness, and compassion, it is because that love, compassion, and kindness resides with us. If you notice beauty, it is because you are that beauty.

If a monster lives inside each of us, what might that monster need? If unconditional love is what we are made of, how do we activate that and fully bring it to the world? If we are truly beings of light, why not go into the darkest of dark places to illuminate them? This is the work of humanity that leads to knowing the Divine self within us and others.

Namaste is not a word to be thrown around because it looks and sounds good. It is a sacred anointing to be held with the utmost reverence when spoken. It should not be spoken unless embodied; otherwise, such behavior is an expression of artificial lighting that is complicit. This is true for any sacred words or expressions of positivity.

It is for this reason that all signs appear throughout our lives. Signs manifest to tear down the falsehoods you carry. They were initiated the moment you took on your first lie, soaked in your first discordant energy, or held onto the first bit of baggage. They began the first time you claimed to be something other than what you really are.

When resisting presence and participation, your experience wanes, and life shrinks back. Yield a broadened perspective by fully engaging life and every experience it brings. You will not only see how life expresses, but that you are that very expression.

In every moment, you are being called to immerse within life, without getting bogged down in any one experience. Through this, you awaken to the experience of living, being, and knowing yourself as life's longing for itself. Life is experiencing through you.

LIVING RAINBOWS

Life is a-maze-ing… You will weave and wander, get lost and find your way… to get lost again and find another way. Each time you do, you will see more of the world outside yourself as the world within you. Each bump in the road, discordant relationship, and experience is a projection from the movie in your mind. The one you fight is you. The one you love is you, too. Do not mistake what's on the screen of life as real. It is made real through what you project.

Feeling complete with my road trip, I returned to South Carolina. One morning soon after, I woke up at 4:30 am. I had spent a week of reliving the fullness of the Newport experience, writing details in my journal. The early hours of my practice are like deep breaths. I cannot be without them. These moments feel deeply nourishing. On this day, I felt called to venture out earlier than usual for my morning walk.

I was open to a response. I had placed questions for the universe/ Spirit/ God/ Source in my journal. I knew it would only be a matter of time before I received answers, but I felt this response might take longer than usual. I had posed a big question.

I was barely out for twenty minutes when a large sign surprised me. The universe's response was undeniable, miraculous, and symbolic. I was astounded. A giant, brightly colored, hot-air balloon hovered in the air a short distance from me, about thirty feet in the air. It was colored like a vertical rainbow. A hot air balloon was an unusual sight; this one was extraordinary, magical, and very much out of place.

The balloon began to drop, as if right on cue. It floated along the brilliant azure sky toward me. It appeared weightless. What a gift!

I could not tell if the balloon pilot was attempting to land or having some sort of trouble lifting off. They hovered about ten inches from the lake's surface. A crowd began gathering. The suspense was building. I could not imagine where the balloon came from, how it got out there, or why it was so close to the water.

This sign was meant for me. I was filled with wonder, delight, excitement, joy, and awe. It was beautiful! Its color was brilliant! It produced sensations of ease, lightness, and flight within me.

I closed my eyes, centering the balloon in my heart. My breathing was deep and relaxed. The message soon came.

See how beautiful and light you are? Embrace your unique color and design. You are in the midst of ascension. This is not out of body, but spiritual involution and expansion. To be more embodied. You are designed to rise high and see from overhead. It is more important to remain grounded. The balloon hangs above the water to remind that you must stay close to your elements. It is important to feel. Humanity has an ocean of emotion to dissolve.

View life from the perspective of "on high." Peer down on all experiences and circumstances as if looking from overhead, from the lens of the Divine. However, live at the surface and receive your full humanity. Float in the mastery that you have achieved. Flourish where you are. Continue to rise as you are invited into the experiences being offered to you. Do not fear the changes taking place, as these are for your highest good at this time. If any frequency pulls at your energy, rise above.

Everything will come together in perfect ways. You will be in the right places at the right times. You no longer need to descend beneath the waters, if doing the work regularly. Time in deep water was necessary. Rise now. From all you gathered within the basking of humanity, be the example. Write what you know, and let it go. Now fly.

Just then, the balloon began to lift. Whatever reason they had for hanging so low shifted and they took off.

I am delighted by rainbows. Since then, I have embraced seeing all human beings as rainbow bodies. I watched the balloon soar and gently meander across the sky. It was amazing! It felt like Oz. I had the feeling of coming home. There is no place like home.

SIGNS OF TRANSCENDENCE

Stages of insight and awareness occur with deepening self-inquiry, contemplation, and introspection. The trek from forgetting to remembering is an experiential process. Through grit and grace, original innocence remains accessible. Although full realization can take a great deal of time, through commitment, diligence, and devotion, it is possible to rediscover the whole self. Self-love is the most important ingredient.

As veils continually thin, the touchstones that the universe, the soul, and life present become more accessible. An ever-expanding upward and downward spiral of living, being, and knowing paves the way toward every human being experiencing material growth, personal growth, and spiritual growth.

Experience has taught me of the rhythmic and cyclical nature of life. More profoundly, I am now aware of how life echoes in time loops, bringing certain signs back around for a deepening spiral of involution and expression. Through what has been shared, I do hope you are beginning to gain an understanding as well. Sink deeply into the subtlest of life's whispers.

The Universe keeps smiling upon us. Not a day goes by without its mystical guidance. The cosmos has a compassionate, kind, and gentle touch. Life has shown me that nothing is personal, unless made to be. Everything is energy that continually attempts to rebalance itself—while also balancing you, me, us, them, and our world.

At the right and perfect time, a new question will rise along your path: Am I here for my ego, or for my soul? This question of discernment appears as a three-way fork in the road. Discerning what each of these paths mean is based upon how you hear and what you perceive as experience and expression. Mind you, there is no right or wrong. These are levels of consciousness that bring forward a specific vibrational reflection of signs, symbols, and synchronicity relative to each person.

One path leads to all that your ego craves, but this is often directly opposite the soul's mission and fulfillment. It is a life created by the unconscious, wounded self, and it lives on the surface of life. This is not necessarily fulfilling, as it is based in craving and desire. This path focuses on the external. Poverty, drought, and emptiness reflect the consciousness of separation and hierarchy that is deeply held within the body. This is a path of material growth.

The second is a path of soul fulfillment. It follows a saga of humanity that has been building lifetime after lifetime. On this road, the ego serves the soul for identity to be used well. In these times, most people are being directed to follow the voice of the soul and learn how to use the ego in ways that enhance its mission of healing. This offers a middle path of balance within the world of form. Here, life moves according to the intertwining shadows and light of the multidimensional layers of self, including one's ancestry and generational heritage. This is a path for healing all that has been collected and karmically accrued. Those born through Generation Z generally fall within this spectrum. This is a path of personal growth.

The third is the path of the unknown, where ego and soul continually surrender all desires, cravings, needs, and wants for the ultimate experience of transcendence. Some beings who express as autistic, transgender, and nonbinary represent stages leading toward this level of consciousness. These phases of human expansion are leading toward androgyny and a sign of the return home. They illustrate the transition toward the Divine immersion and merging of masculine and feminine. Those who fall within Generations Alpha and early Betas are part of this transitional phase of beings, each in their own expression.

Generations Beta (the latter spectrum) and Gamma will express and embody the new Divine human who can hold transcendence. They will not only possess a capacity for conscious presence, but also utilize a greater extent of the three brains embedded within our human body technology. This is when humanity will begin to reclaim Divine mastery. This unknown is a path of spiritual growth.

In deeply intimate conversations, you can be led to wisdom that delights you privately or may be shared with the world. What matters most is your connection to self, Spirit, and living life in a manner that fulfills you. Inner unity raises individual minds to levels of consciousness that culminate in higher collective resonance, ultimately producing a field of common sentience.

My life is a sign to trust what you receive. It is an example of how signs spread across decades until you realize that *you* are a sacred encounter. You are a pathway. You are a Divine guidepost. You are the turning point. It is all *you*… each sign, every symbol, and all synchronicities. Your sacred stories and mystical experiences are jewels for collective awareness and awakening.

I gained this understanding step-by-step, from the moment I was aware enough to embark upon personal growth.

THE FABRIC OF REALITY

•———— • ◉ ◕ ◔ • ———— •

*L*ife is a magical kingdom, where the random, seemingly insignificant, and earthly unite. Each has a place and purpose in your dialogue with the cosmos. Give yourself the experience of partnership with the universe. Awaken your ability to be in full receivership. Be used well by life. This communion is available to anyone and to all. No special skill is required. Remain open, curious, and in conversation. Be willing to engage in self inquiry.

You can embark upon each day as if no magic exists in the world, or you can choose to live as if every single thing in the world is magical. Grounding within the latter opens you to a world filled with mystical wonder and grace-filled generosity. The entire world is at your disposal and waiting to be experienced. You exist in continual partnership with life.

Your soul longs for you to prove this to yourself by becoming an example of magic and mystery. Your journey is bearing witness to this. You are cellularly driven to experientially discover that life is not random... that all things are connected... and that you are able to find yourself within everything that manifests in the world. You were born to seek and make meaning of what seems meaningless.

You will experience much that is unexpected, yet everything encountered is built into the storyline that was designed to unfold for you. Earth is a land of opposites. It provides a palpable texture and unique subtleties for engaging the human experience. Life is filled with contrast. The polarity of light and dark serves as the background for this journey of a lifetime.

Embedded within each individual's story, the soul has placed a trail of breadcrumbs to guide the way out of slumber and into the wakeful awareness of remembrance. Although constriction may seem to occur along the way, infinite essence is always, and only, expanding. Life avails itself of everything possible to be utilized as messages for you.

Reality is like a textured cloth, undulating with the warping of darkness and weaving of light within the cosmic loom. Within these interlacing ribbons, the golden thread of essence shines through with the rich sparkle of synchronicity—and a shimmering trail of signs. It is all light; everything is. Through its varying shades and hues, the texture of life can be felt, experienced, and fully imbibed.

As each moment loops into the next, life shapes the garment that becomes your experience. By utilizing the signs and symbols that life presents, you adorn your sacred cloth with the embellishments of delight, awe, and joy. These shiny sequins and crystals are spread throughout your experience. If you are willing to see, each one is a guidepost.

See what you may not have noticed before. There exists a partnership within life that you have not yet fully realized, nor utilized. Within the context of your experience is a way to fully trust again. This will enable you to rediscover your true power, inner authority, and Divine creative capacity. When you do so, an entirely new set of signs—mystical encounters, Divine guideposts, and turning points—will unfold. Enjoy the ride. All that is ever required is curiosity, willingness, and a sense of adventure.

Within each moment of experience, nothing is separate. Each part requires every other to be a whole experience. A flower cannot have fragrance without the engagement of someone inhaling scent. A mountain cannot be regal without being gazed upon. A puppy cannot be soft and sweet without a presence to witness, hold, and caress it. You are that experiencing. All else is appearing so that experience can experience itself.

The universe will not speak so clearly that you become complacent and disinterested, but in a way that beckons exploration, creativity, and artistry. You have been born unto life as an arrow of curiosity, divination, and musing. You are the perspective of wonder that life longs to know.

The world is speaking to you. Life is a calling. Your soul is beckoning. In the most quiet moments, you already see, feel, or hear this. Your life is speaking loudly in more ways than you can imagine. Embrace your entire experience as the journey of a lifetime, as you unfold the fabric of your reality. You are a golden thread weaving itself into the wondrous.

Expand your conversations with the universe... your dialogue with signs... and a unique dialect with the Divine. Let your sacred encounters lead to destined Divine guideposts, turning points, and pathways. Every phase of your journey will be unique, each holding layers of multidimensionality. Your signs, symbols, and messages are equally so. The universe is your loving companion and co-creator.

Every person has embedded within themselves a sacred moment when the soul says, "It's time to turn within and know you are already home." Each sign, symbol, and synchronicity is a ticking of that clock . . . until the individual chooses to wake up. There is not one thing in life that does not offer that remembrance and gateway to truth in an intensely soulful and personal way.

You came for mastery. You came for the embodied experience of living, being, and knowing as Experience, experiencing itself. You are the journey. Most importantly, you are light that shines within darkness.

Good wishes and great love...

Simran

MEET OUR SACRED STORYTELLERS

MARINA ALZUGARAY, MSN is a Curandera Partera pioneer of water births, a passioned activist of "Birth in love for every family and love for birth in every setting." Midwife Marina is currently mentoring a new generation of holistic community midwives. midwifemarina.com.

HAYLEY BARKLA is a credible channeler and has stepped beyond the confinement of corporate life into her true passion of raising spiritual self-awareness and expanding conscious creation through her vlog and personal readings.

MARY-ELIZABETH BRISCOE, LCMHC, CAGCS is the founder of Integrated Grief Works, LLC and the award-winning author of *The First Signs of April: A Memoir on Grief and Healing*. integratedgriefworks.com.

ANNE CEDERBERG is a Naturalist and artist, specializing in mystical nature experiences and the healing power of nature. Her mission is to help others see God in nature. ourmysticalnature.wordpress.com.

V.L. CESSNA lives in Northeast Ohio with her two amazing gifts from God, her husband and son. She is a financial executive and people leader, CPA,

CMA, IIN Health Coach, writer, and cancer survivor. V.L. is a contributor to Living Well U and the founder of Enuff Is Enuff, helping others live their best life. enuffisenuff.com.

PATRICIA EWERS is from a small fishing village in Jamaica West Indies. She came to the United States at the age of fourteen. Patricia is a first-grade teacher in Brooklyn, New York and the mother of two amazing children.

BARBARA ROSS GREANEY is an ordained minister of the Universal Brotherhood, spiritual counselor, holistic healer, and inspirational writer. She provides spiritual counseling, holistic healing, and channeling. Barbara lives in Leesburg, Florida. reverendbarb.com.

DR. JOANNE HALVERSON lived off-grid in the woods. Coast Salish shamans entrusted her with initiations, wisdom, and medicine names-Ancient Spirit Person and Sikahtahlia. Such gifts are to be shared. thrivecounselorseattle. com.

EMILY HINE is a technology, mental health, and mindfulness entrepreneur. She is a Compassion Teacher and author of the forthcoming book *Holy Sit: Learning to Sit, Stay, Heal, and Serve.* emilyhine.com.

ANN MARIE HOLMES is an author, Feng Shui specialist, and Earth intuitive. She created a five-acre nature sanctuary and school about sacred earth living. She lives in Kapaa, Hawaii. earthspiritspaces.com.

JOANNA KAZMIROWICZ emigrated to Australia from Poland at the age of 26 with her husband and child. She worked as a clinical nurse and loves reading, fashion, ceramics, gardening, and traveling.

KHEPERA SEK KM seeks peace in her everyday existence and finds it in nature, at the ocean, and within sacred connections. As a birth doula she is honored to support women during birth and feels blessed to witness a soul's arrival.

TAMARA KNOX M.MSC, D.D. is an international bestselling author and devotee to the Light. She seeks truth and insight through the Amnion—a fluid domain shown to her by Archangels Sandalphon and Gabriel. shekinahpath.com.

JOANNA LAI is a teacher and a dreamer. Having read English at university, she spends her time deepening her relationship with the Divine through writing.

JENNY MANNION is an author, speaker, teacher, and healer inspiring self-love and tools to manifest the life we desire. Healing herself of seven years of diseases in three weeks awakened her to her passion and purpose of helping others. jennymannion.com.

DR. BONNIE MCLEAN is a retired RN, current Acupuncture Physician, Doctor of Oriental Medicine, author, and speaker. She has practiced her healing work for a total of 50 years. spiritgatemedicine.com.

PAMELA D. NANCE has a master's in cultural anthropology, minor degrees in archaeology and religion, and a 30 year career in social and biostatistical sciences. Pamela has researched the survival of consciousness after death for over 30 years and obtained certifications in healing touch, past life regression, shamanism, and spiritual dowsing. pamelanance.com.

ELIZABETH PAROJCIC is a popular and respected intuitive guide and spiritual teacher. With hundreds of clients internationally, her quest is to teach people to live a more fulfilling life in every aspect; physically, mentally, spiritually, and intuitively. She is a certified Reiki Master, Law of Attraction Practitioner, Crystal Healing Practitioner, and Advanced Sixth Sensory Practitioner. elizabethparojcic.com.

BRIGITTE BARTLEY SAWYER is a mother to three boys, ages 21, 20 and 17 and stepmother to two daughters, ages 17 and 20 and an advocate for nutrition and mindset. Brigitte channeled her passion of nutrition into network marketing with now an organization of 110,000+ associates. Her passion for supporting small business led her to social media marketing with clients across the country. brigittebartley.com.

JENNIFER PEREZ SOLAR is a Samassati Colorlight practitioner, newborn care specialist, and teacher. Her psychic and mediumship gifts merge with her business expertise to show others how to be change agents and movement creators. She hosts spiritual retreats to encourage others to learn the power of their own intuition through the frequency of color. allowandflow.com.

MARYANN SUSSONI is a former educator of creative arts, theater, and writing in NYC. Since childhood she has had an affinity for the creative arts and she has been writing for as long as she can remember.

AGUSTINA THORGILSSON is a licensed psychologist. Her vision is to help the world by showing people how to transcend even the most difficult life-experiences they can encounter and find peace. lifenavigation.com.

YOLANDA TONG is a Melbourne Australia based Voice Channeler who supports intuitives, healers, and wellness practitioners to develop their unique gifts and grow into their potential. yolandatong.com.

MEET OUR FEATURED AUTHOR

SIMRAN is a globally recognized speaker and catalyst for love, compassion, and humanity. As an "Example" for a New World Experience of Aliveness, she advocates for the visionary and mystical embodied within each person. SIMRAN steers individuals toward the embrace of their darkest depths, to uncover their brilliance of light for the purposes of attaining true wholeness, personal power, and peace.

SIMRAN is a #1 rated, archived and syndicated host of *Voice America's 11:11 Talk Radio*; host of *11:11 InnerViews TV*; and publisher of the Nautilus Award-winning *11:11 Magazine*. SIMRAN is the author of the *Self-Realization Trilogy* consisting of (1) *LIVING: The 7 Blessings of Human Experience*, (2) *BEING: The 7 Illusions That Derail Personal Power, Purpose and Peace*, and (3) *KNOWING: The 7 Human Expressions of Grace*; in addition to her first trilogy of self-awareness consisting of (1) IPPY and IPA Gold Award-winning *Conversations With The Universe*; (2) *Your Journey to Enlightenment*; and

(3) IPPY Gold Award-winning *Your Journey to Love*. SIMRAN creates art, books, and online courses to bridge humanity's experience and expression. Along with being a TEDx speaker, SIMRAN is the creator of the *One-Woman Show, The Rebel Road... Connecting the Dots from What Was to What Is.*

SIMRAN has appeared on GAIAM TV, One Word Puja Network, CCN, and The New Thought Channel. Her *11:11 Talk Radio* show appears on Voice America Network and DreamVisions7Radio Network along with other syndications. She has appeared as keynote speaker at The World Congress, the United Nations, universities, spiritual centers and hundreds of venues across North America. Along with having been featured on the covers of *Science of Mind Magazine, Jolie Magazine,* and *The Owl Magazine,* SIMRAN is also a recipient of the "UnZipper of Reality" Award.

SIMRAN has two sons and resides in Charleston, South Carolina. Find out more at iamsimran.com or 1111mag.com